Two of Cleveland's most enduring architectural symbols, the Terminal Tower and Cleveland Municipal Stadium, are seen in this 1949 aerial view. The Terminal still stands tall; the Stadium is no more. (Robert Runyon Photo, Bruce Young collection)

Cleveland Stadium:
The Last Chapter

BY JAMES A. TOMAN & GREGORY G. DEEGAN

PUBLISHING INFORMATION

1st edition published as Cleveland Municipal Stadium
©1981 Cleveland Landmarks Press, Inc.

2nd edition published as Cleveland Stadium: Sixty Years of Memories
©1991 Cleveland Landmarks Press, Inc.

Revised edition published
©1994 Cleveland Landmarks Press, Inc.

3rd edition published as Cleveland Stadium: The Last Chapter
©1997 Cleveland Landmarks Press, Inc.

Library of Congress Catalog Card Number: 97-66800

ISBN: 0-936760-10-9
Published by Cleveland Landmarks Press, Inc.
13610 Shaker Boulevard, Suite 503
Cleveland, Ohio 44120-1592

Printed by Consolidated Graphics Group
Cleveland, Ohio

Cover Photo: © Mort Tucker Photography

Cover Design: Jeffrey A. Slater

Inside Design: Robert Misiolek, Christopher Smith, and Peter Zeller

PREFACE AND ACKNOWLEDGMENTS

This volume marks the fourth time that Cleveland Landmarks Press has published a book detailing the history and stories of Cleveland Municipal Stadium. The original edition appeared in 1981, commemorating the golden anniversary of the lady by the lake. It was updated in 1991, to celebrate the facility's sixtieth anniversary, and then revised again in 1994, after the Indians left the Stadium in 1993. This 1997 edition (officially the third edition) was produced as the last installment of the Stadium story. Thus, the title.

In the previous books, the Stadium seemed to be a fixed presence on the lakefront whose existence seemed unshakable. Unfortunately, the announcement in Baltimore on November 6, 1995, not only shook Greater Clevelanders but also the seemingly stable foundation upon which the Stadium stood. The outpouring of support for the Stadium by the voters just after the bombshell and the affectionate regard which fans showed to the lady by the lake at the Final Play made it seem to us it was time to tell the Stadium's story one last time.

Cleveland Stadium: The Last Chapter has been completely rewritten. This edition includes an expanded color photo section, many different black-and-white photos from the 1994 edition, an additional chapter on the various plans to renovate the facility that never came to fruition, an updated section detailing the Browns' final seasons at Municipal Stadium, and a chapter telling the sad story of the lakefront park's demolition.

Since this edition was built upon the earlier volumes, we must acknowledge all those who helped make the other editions possible. In particular, we thank Dan Cook, who co-authored the first edition and has supported all of the subsequent efforts. We also thank Dino Lucarelli, longtime employee of Cleveland Stadium Corporation and the Cleveland Browns; it was his idea in the first place to have a book written about the Stadium. We are also grateful to the late Ed Uhas, public relations director for Cleveland Stadium Corporation, who assisted with the previous two books and who carefully tended the Stadium's archives.

Mike Poplar, former executive vice president of the Cleveland Stadium Corporation, and Bruce Gaines, its former director of building services, deserve our special thanks. Their longtime devotion and service to the Stadium prompted them to encourage us to write this volume. Throughout the project, their valuable insights and guidance were ever available to us.

We also owe gratitude to many others who contributed to this project. First, from the Cleveland Indians, we express thanks to Susie Gharrity and Curtis Danberg and to Frank Derry and Linda DeCarlo at *Indians Ink*. Ray Yannucci at *Browns News Illustrated* assisted us in various ways. Thanks as well go to Morris Eckhouse and Joe Simenic of the Society of American Baseball Research (SABR), and to Mike Brown of the Cincinnati Bengals. Thanks also to Dryck Bennett.

We gathered photos from many sources, and hopefully we have credited them correctly. Apologies to anyone whose work may have been accidentally misidentified. We acknowledge the assistance of Bill Becker, Cleveland State University Archives; May Perencevic of Cleveland Public Library; Jack Muslovski, Bruce Young, Jim Spangler, David Kachinko, Blaine Hays, Mike Speranza, Paul Tepley, Bill Nehez, Skip Trombetti, and Mort Tucker for their original work or for sharing their collections with us.

Finally, a personal thanks for the support of the Deegans, Carmosinos, and especially Liz Fay. As always, it meant the world.

To all we acknowledge our debt. This book is the result of real collaboration. Its strengths are due to the generosity of our helpers. Its weaknesses are our own.

James A. Toman and Gregory G. Deegan

INTRODUCTION

First came baseball. Then came football. There was even an occasional soccer ball. Finally, however, there came the wrecking ball, and Cleveland Municipal Stadium disappeared from the scene.

This book is the fourth in a series which have chronicled the history of Cleveland Municipal Stadium. Like its predecessors, it begins with the events which led to the original planning for the giant edifice on the lakefront. Unlike them, however, it ends with the Stadium's demolition, a fate that seemed unthinkable—or at least unlikely—just three years ago when the last edition was published.

And, of course, this volume covers much that happened along the way between construction and demolition. It is these events which permit the Stadium to live on in the memories of the millions who at one time or another passed through its gates, sat in its seats, and took in some kind of spectacle.

Why did the final curtain call finally come for the grand old gal on the lakefront? It will take the perspective of time for that question to be adequately answered. But in a global way, the answer is relatively simple. Changing social circumstances rendered the Stadium obsolete. In an age when professional sports became a multi-billion dollar business, and when luxurious appointments and status-symbol perquisites were deemed necessary to lure the well-heeled crowd, the simple designs and time-honored amenities which Cleveland Stadium offered could no longer compete. The Stadium simply could not generate the kind of revenues required by today's sports empires.

Perhaps there was a time when the Stadium could have been saved. Certainly there were plans aplenty, and even a 1995 vote by Greater Clevelanders to authorize financing for the Stadium's renovation. But by the time those pieces were finally in place, it was too late. The Indians' had moved to Gateway, and the Browns were hijacked to Baltimore. The planned multi-million dollar renovation of Cleveland Stadium could not meet the exacting criteria of the National Football League to award the city a new franchise. And so the old Stadium's fate was sealed.

Cleveland Municipal Stadium was not an architectural gem. Last-minute cutbacks on its ornamentation prevented that kind of stature. Its demise, then, does not deprive the city of a landmark distinguished by its design charms.

But something maybe even more important is gone. The Stadium was a repository of memories. Legendary heroes of baseball and football walked across its field. Brilliant victories and heartwrenching defeats were played out there. From the rostrums of civic events and the pulpits of religious ones came inspiration and edification. The field that presented these spectacles is now gone, and the aura of tradition and history which the passage of time brought to it has disappeared with it.

Many will remember first visiting the Stadium's cavernous interior as children, brought by dad and/or mom for their first taste of big league baseball or football. Others will fondly recall those bonding rituals of adolescence and young adulthood, when Cleveland Stadium meant rock-n-roll on the grand scale. Return visits to the Stadium meant not only experiencing the new but recharging memories of the old. Now that opportunity no longer exists.

Now the Stadium has disappeared, and people will have to remember as best they can. If this volume helps in any way, it will have done what it was meant to do.

CITY PLANNING AND THE LAKEFRONT

1

The City of Cleveland celebrated the centennial of its founding in 1896. To mark the anniversary, the city fathers had a giant triumphal arch constructed across Superior Avenue on Public Square, just east of Ontario Street. Near that arch, as well as across the community, a series of civic observances celebrated a century of rapid population growth and industrial expansion for the city. Cleveland had much to celebrate. The next census would officially show that Cleveland had become the largest city in the State of Ohio and the seventh largest in the nation.

In 1896 Cleveland marked its centennial by erecting a giant wooden arch over Superior Avenue in Public Square. The City was not yet ready to embark on an ambitious program of public building. (Western Reserve Historical Society collection)

At the end of the centennial year, city workers dismantled the arch. It had been built from wood, and it had been meant only as a temporary monument. The City of Cleveland had not yet reached the point when it was fully ready to mark its maturity with monuments that would endure. That phase in the city's life was not long in coming, however. It got underway during the administration of Cleveland's most famous mayor, Tom L. Johnson, who led the City between 1901 and 1909.

Until Johnson's term in office, the city's rapid growth had been more organic than planned. Cleveland's public buildings gave evidence of the haphazard nature of its development. The Cuyahoga County Court House on Public Square was a dingy and nondescript building which already had been expanded twice to meet the needs of an increasing population. The City of Cleveland itself did not even own its center of operations; city business was conducted from rented quarters in the Case Block at East Third Street and Superior Avenue. The closest the city had to a facility where significant numbers of its citizens could assemble was the privately owned Arcade on Euclid Avenue and East Fourth Street. Cleveland Public Library's main downtown headquarters was also without a permanent home, and its location shifted as changing circumstances dictated.

Knowing that a great city could and should do better, in 1899 the Cleveland Chamber of Commerce began to campaign for construction of the kind of government center that would befit Cleveland's growing national stature.

Three years later, on June 20, 1902, Mayor Johnson took the first steps to give form to the Chamber of Commerce vision. He appointed three nationally known urban architects, Daniel H. Burnham, Arnold R. Brunner, and John M. Carrere, to design a master plan to give Cleveland a proud and permanent civic center. Except for Washington, D.C., no other city in the nation was prepared to plan on so grand a scale. Just over one year later, on August 17, 1903, the findings of the distinguished panel were made public. Their recommendations came to be known as the Group Plan.

The Group Plan covered 104 acres of downtown land running north from Superior Avenue to the lakefront, between Public Square and East Sixth Street. East Third Street would serve as the north-south axis. The street would be replaced by a park, the plan's centerpiece. The mall, as this park would be known, would be 560 feet wide and stretch from Rockwell Avenue to the bluff overlooking the railroad tracks that traversed the lakefront. The perimeter of this lavishly landscaped mall would be lined with stately public buildings, giving the city a lasting and architecturally distinguished government center. The Group Plan met with critical acclaim, and soon thereafter work was underway to convert the concept into reality.

In 1905 construction began at the southern end of the Mall for the United States Post Office, Customs House, and Court House (today referred to as the old Federal Court House). It was completed in 1910. Other buildings were soon to follow. In 1912 came the Cuyahoga County Court House, and in 1916 Cleveland City Hall, straddling the Mall at Lakeside Avenue. Public Auditorium, along the eastern side of the Mall, between Lakeside and St. Clair avenues, came on line in 1922. Three years later Cleveland Public Library's new home joined the Federal Court House to complete the Mall's southern boundary. In 1930 the Cleveland Board of Education Building, along the eastern Mall line between St. Clair and Rockwell avenues, opened for business.

Not until 1933 was the Mall itself completed. In that year the underground exhibition hall was completed, the remaining structures blighting the Mall's expanse were cleared away, and its formal landscaping was finished.

Not every element of the original Group Plan, however, was carried out. One key provision in the master plan had been to build a new union railroad station at the Mall's northern end, directly over the lakefront tracks. It would replace the 1866-vintage Union Depot at the foot of West Ninth Street and consolidate all the railroad's passenger operations, then divided among several separate stations, under one roof.

Soon the site for the new railroad depot was mired in controversy. While the city fathers fought to protect the plan for the lakefront union station, opposition came from Oris Paxton and Mantis James Van Sweringen. The brothers owned land at the southwest quadrant of Public Square and wanted the station to be built there, where it could also serve as the passenger terminal for their planned network of rapid transit lines. The location issue, the lakefront versus Public Square, was eventually put into the voters' hands, and on January 10, 1919, they decided in favor of the Van Sweringen plan. That decision created a void in the Group Plan's design for the lakefront and created the need to bring some other civic construction to the Mall's northern perimeter.

While construction went on along the more southerly portions of the Mall district, planners continued to envision the importance of the lakefront itself. The land area to the north of the lakefront railroad trackage was continually expanded with fill. During the 1920s alone, some 300,000 car loads of fill material were dumped along the lakefront, chiefly between West Ninth and East 12th streets, thrusting the shoreline ever farther into Lake Erie. While some Clevelanders viewed the filling operation as little more than a convenient dump site and deplored the situation, nonetheless land was being created that would someday permit a rebirth of the City's lakefront.

In 1928 the Terminal Tower was completed, moving the site for the city's union railroad station from the planned lakefront site to Public Square. The area originally intended for the facility was ready for alternative development. (Jim Spangler collection)

When construction finally began on the Cleveland Union Terminal project on Public Square in late 1919, city officials realized that development along the Group Plan's northern boundary would have to be reconceptualized. It was not until 1923, however, that the idea of using the site for a stadium first surfaced, and that idea originated not with city planners but with an administrator for the Cleveland City School District. Floyd A. Rowe, the district's supervisor for health and physical

Two key figures in bringing about construction of a stadium on the lakefront were E. S. Barnard, president of the Cleveland Indians, 1922-1926 (top); and William R. Hopkins, city manager 1924-1930 (bottom). (Cleveland Press Collection of the Cleveland State University Archives)

education, suggested that a lakefront stadium, with a 20,000-25,000 seating capacity, would be an ideal venue for high school football games. He outlined his ideas for the plan with Cleveland Mayor Fred Kohler on September 18, 1923. Without ready funds for the project, however, neither the city nor the school district assigned the concept a high priority, and consequently the plan languished. Nonetheless, the seeds of an idea had been planted.

In 1921 Cleveland voters decided to reinvent city government by adopting a city-manager form of governance. The new system went into effect in January 1924, and William R. Hopkins was the first to serve the City from the city-manager's chair. A strong leader with a background in development, Hopkins took the next steps to filling the void on the lakefront. Spurred by a suggestion from City Councilman Peter Witt, in 1926 Hopkins asked P. P. Evans, president of Osborn Engineering Company, to draw up preliminary plans for a lakefront stadium. He had in mind a facility which could seat 80,000-100,000, with a construction budget in the vicinity of $2 million.

With a conceptual design in hand for the new stadium, Hopkins then met with Ernest S. Barnard, since 1922 president of the Cleveland Indians baseball club. At the time Barnard was running the club on behalf of the widow of the former owner, "Sunny Jim" Dunn who had died in 1922. He was then in the process of trying to find a new owner for the Indians.

At the time the Cleveland Indians were playing in their own baseball park at East 66th Street and Lexington Avenue. Earlier and later known as League Park, the facility was then named Dunn Field for its recent owner. Barnard had mixed feelings about the advisability of moving the team from its own property to a municipally owned one, but he also recognized that Dunn Field had its limitations. Despite a grandstand extension in 1919, the park could only seat 22,000 fans, the smallest capacity in the league. A larger stadium could make the franchise more attractive to potential buyers.

Barnard soon found himself pressed for time. Besides searching for a new team owner, he was also preparing himself for the duties he would soon assume as president of baseball's American League. Despite the time constraints, Barnard consulted regularly with Osborn officials in refining plans for the lakefront stadium, and he continued his collaborative efforts even after he left Cleveland. Later, K. H.

This preliminary sketch for Cleveland Stadium was prepared for the civic committee trying to convince Clevelanders to vote in favor of bonds for the lakefront park. The sketch bears marked similarities to the Los Angeles Coliseum. (Osborn Engineering Company)

Osborn, who was ultimately responsible for the stadium's final design, reported that its configuration had "evolved from a study of the ideal Baseball Grandstand." Barnard also found the team a new owner. Alva Bradley took over the franchise in November 1927.

Times were different then, and cities were not yet in the habit of subsidizing their professional sports franchises. Most baseball clubs owned their facilities. The idea of becoming a tenant in a city-owned ballpark represented relatively new ground. Still, Bradley knew that he needed a larger stadium, and his interest in purchasing the team had been buoyed by plans for the new lakefront facility. In April 1928, perhaps to prompt the City to action, Bradley talked about his own Stadium plans at a Builders' Exchange forum. Bradley told the audience, "If the city doesn't provide a stadium, as we hope it will, we will lease the land and build it....No big city is really a big city unless it has a stadium."

The city fathers, however, were viewing the new stadium as a potential profit maker, and Bradley's statement that the Indians might be willing to build their own facility prodded the City into renewed action. In 1928 a new Group Plan Commission was established to provide updated guidelines for completing the civic center. A blue-ribbon Cleveland Stadium Committee was also established, chaired by businessman Charles A. Otis.

The Group Plan Commission essentially faced the question of how to complete the Mall plan by filling the space once reserved for the railroad station. In place of the

One scheme for the Group Plan called for connecting the upper mall to the waterfront by means of a terraced walkway. A stadium and a municipal swimming pool would occupy the area north of the railroad tracks. (Cleveland Press Collection of the Cleveland State University Archives)

station, the Commission recommended that a terrace be constructed over the lakefront railroad tracks, to extend the green way of the Mall to the water's edge. Balancing this park-like extension would be two structures. On the western boundary, at West Third Street, the new stadium could be built. The eastern end could serve as the site for either a large exhibition hall or for a municipal swimming pool. Otis's stadium committee endorsed the recommendation, and the plans went before City Council in August 1928. On August 21, with only one dissenting vote, City Council authorized a $2.5 million bond issue to be put before the voters on the November ballot.

The campaign to gain voter support then went into high gear. While plans for the Stadium had been drawn primarily with the idea in mind to create an ideal baseball facility, the campaign itself did not focus on professional sports. The

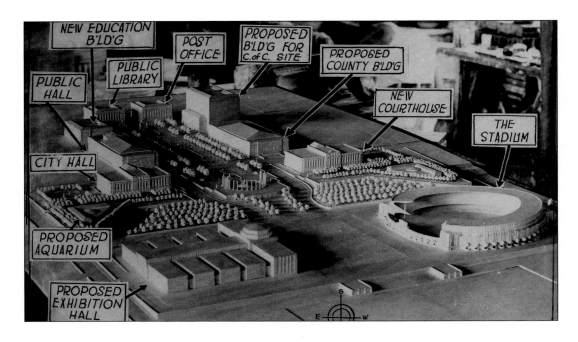

The model shows one concept for the Group Plan for downtown Cleveland. In this scheme, a stadium is joined on the waterfront by an exhibition hall. (Cleveland Public Library collection)

literature produced by the committee stated that the city needed the Stadium "as a symbol of civic progress and pride," and that the building would add to the Group Plan and thus serve as a "token that Cleveland is a great city."

The Stadium was promoted as a multi-purpose facility, and Otis's committee cited some 60 different activities to which the new building could be home. Among the uses were: pageants, dramatic offerings, musical entertainments, civic gatherings, business expositions, along with sporting events. In the latter category, the committee suggested that the Stadium would be ideal for boxing, wrestling, gymnastics, track and field, skating, hockey, tennis, soccer, and even cricket, as well as the old standbys of baseball and football. These athletic events were meant to cover the entire gamut from local scholastic contests to national amateur ones, and from collegiate to professional sports.

Various design changes are reflected in this revised sketch for the Stadium which closely corresponds to the final drawings. (Cleveland Public Library collection)

City Planning and the Lakefront

In later days, the myth would arise that Cleveland Stadium had been built in the hopes of hosting the 1932 Olympic Games. Nothing in the planning or engineering records, in the speeches of William Hopkins, in the newspaper clippings of the day, or in the literature used in the voter campaign indicate that the Olympics were anything more than a talking point to describe just how versatile the lakefront facility would be. On the contrary, the Stadium was built primarily to meet the needs of the city's professional baseball team. Having a huge facility for public events was also seen as putting Cleveland in the same "league" as Chicago and Philadelphia, which commissioned major outdoor arenas. The Stadium was meant to give Cleveland continuing status, to demonstrate to the nation that Cleveland was anything but a second-tier metropolis. That was a purpose far more enduring than a short summer of Olympic Games.

The words of the advertising director for the campaign, James L. Hubbell, probably describe the intent best:

> The new stadium, when erected and in operation, will add immeasurably to the attraction of Cleveland as a great city. For many years to come it will stand as a monument to a progressive spirit and as an expression of the enterprise that separates successful communities from those which stand still or slowly fall backward in the march of progress.

That kind of argument was what helped Clevelanders make up their minds when they went to the polls on November 6, 1928. The Stadium bond issue required a 55% percent affirmative vote, but voters gave an even more favorable verdict. The issue passed by a comfortable 3-2 margin, 112,448 for and 76,975 against.

Clevelanders had voted to keep faith with the maxim of Daniel Burnham, who had helped shape the original Group Plan. He had counseled: "Make no little plans; they have no magic to stir men's blood..." A massive Cleveland Municipal Stadium would soon rise as the next affirmation of a city which continued to think on the grand scale.

In 1930 landfill activity continues east of East Ninth Street, but the Cleveland Stadium site is nearly ready. (Cleveland Public Library collection)

2

BUILDING ON THE FAST TRACK

Legal hurdles are not new to the process of urban planning and development, and public projects have long seemed to attract a disproportionate share of them. Although the voters had expressed their approval of the new lakefront facility in November 1928, there had been some significant voices raised in opposition to the project, including a select committee of the Cleveland Chamber of Commerce. After the voters had approved the financing for the Stadium, the opposition had only one recourse available to stymie the project, and that was the courtroom. When planning for the mammoth Stadium job was nearing completion in spring 1929, the last battle was joined, and Cleveland Stadium issues moved from the drawing board to the court docket.

On May 29, 1929, Clevelander Andrew Meyer filed a taxpayer suit in Cuyahoga County Common Pleas Court to block the Stadium project. His suit raised several issues. Some of the complaints were technical, referring to the manner in which Cleveland City Council had worded the enabling ordinances for the project. More substantially, he charged that the city had dubious title to the land, an argument which the City thought it had settled when it traded land with the lakefront railroads. The City exchanged a parcel farther west of West Third Street for a piece of land needed for the Stadium site. Meyer also charged that the bonds approved by the voters would be inadequate to pay for the project, nor would future revenues from Stadium operations be sufficient to redeem those bonds, objections which the Chamber of Commerce had aired earlier. He also claimed that the new Stadium failed to qualify as a legitimate public purpose, since it represented the use of public funds primarily to enhance the private well-being of the Cleveland Indians baseball club.

City of Cleveland lawyers spent the next year in court. They successfully defended the City's position in Common Pleas Court, then in the Sixth District Court of Appeals in Cincinnati, and finally before the Ohio Supreme Court. When on April 30, 1930, Ohio's highest court refused to review the Appellate Court's decision, the last legal obstacle was hurdled, and the way was finally cleared for construction to begin.

There had been some last-minute political wrangling over the Stadium as well. City Manager Daniel E. Morgan, who had replaced William R. Hopkins on January 27, 1930, was dissatisfied with the site that Hopkins had selected for the Stadium. Morgan felt that the building should be centered at the northern end of the Mall, rather than near West Third Street. His suggested location, however, would have

prevented subsequent development on the proposed municipal swimming pool or exhibit hall which had been recommended for the eastern end of the lakefront site. Eventually Morgan's concerns were satisfied by having the Stadium's footprint moved only 100 feet farther east.

Before construction could start, it was necessary to extend the Stadium site farther into Lake Erie, September 1930. (Cleveland Public Library collection)

While the lawyers were waging their legal battle and the politicians were debating the project's ideal site, planners were busy putting the finishing touches on the design documents. Two Cleveland firms were the principals involved in the undertaking. Osborn Engineering Company, which had earlier worked with E. S. Barnard on basic concepts for the ideal baseball facility, was signed as the project engineer. The architectural firm of Walker and Weeks was hired as the consulting architect. Both firms came to the project with impressive credentials.

The partnership of Frank R. Walker and Harry E. Weeks had been on the Cleveland scene since 1911. Former employees of the J. Milton Dyer architectural firm in Cleveland, the partners had focused on the design of public buildings. Chief among their accomplishments were two Group Plan buildings along the Mall, Public Auditorium (1922) and Cleveland Public Library (1925), as well as the nearby Federal Reserve Bank Building on Superior Avenue (1923). In 1928 the partners were working on plans for Severance Hall. Their close involvement with the Group Plan made them a natural choice for Stadium consulting architect.

Frank C. Osborn founded the Osborn Engineering Company in Cleveland in 1892, and it quickly earned a respected reputation in the field of athletic facility design. By the time Osborn Engineering was signed on for the Municipal Stadium project, the company had already some 75 sports complexes nationwide to its credit. Among its most famous achievements were Fenway Park in Boston, Comiskey Park in Chicago, and Yankee Stadium in New York City. The company was also responsible for the engineering in some important downtown structures, the Rose Building (1901) and Citizens Building (1902) among them.

Cleveland's W. J. Schirmer Company was named the Stadium's general contractor, and dozens of subcontractors, mostly local companies, were soon signed

The Stadium site required leveling before work could begin on the building's foundation. The scene dates from summer 1930. (Cleveland Public Library collection)

for their portions of the project. Chief among the subcontractors were: Great Lakes Dredge and Dock Company for bulkheading, Fifth City Excavating Company for grading, the Frederick Snare Corporation for foundation work, Bass Construction Company for steel erection, the John Weenink & Sons Company for roof work, the Kahn Company for plumbing, and Parker Electric Company for wiring.

As the various subcontractors submitted their bids, it soon became apparent that the approved budget of $2.5 million was in jeopardy. Foundation, bulkheading, and roadway work were all coming in higher than expected, and the City also had to pay the legal bills it had incurred when defending the project in court. Of course, inadequate financing had been one of the charges that Stadium opponents had raised; they were certain that the Stadium could not be built for the voter-approved sum. To avoid the embarrassment of having to acknowledge that the opponents had been correct in their assessment, City Manager Morgan asked both Walker and Weeks and Osborn officials to find ways to trim costs. Because the Stadium had been designed as part of the Group Plan, Walker and Weeks had selected its external features to complement the existing structures on the bluff above, and therefore original plans had called for the Stadium to be faced in stone. To protect the budget, though, Walker and Weeks changed the exterior finish to a less expensive mix of brick and aluminum. Osborn engineers determined that the single-deck bleacher section did not require the same kind of piling that the rest of the facility needed, and so another cost factor was eliminated. When the architects and engineers had finished their adjustments, the Stadium budget was back on target, with an expected final outlay set at $2,447,657.

Concrete caps were used to crown clusters of piles to provide the foundation for the Stadium's structural steel work. (Cleveland Public Library collection)

Construction work on the Stadium began on June 25, 1930, when the first earth was turned. Because the existing landfill site was unstable and also too narrow for the building, new bulkheading was required, which extended the site 200 feet farther into Lake Erie, and reinforced the site's 1,200 feet of east-west boundary. Then to raise this larger site to eight feet above water level, 100,000 cubic yards of additional fill material were trucked in.

In order to further stabilize the site, 2,521 piles were hammered into the ground, many to a depth of 65 feet. The composite piles of wood and concrete were positioned in clusters, and then joined by a concrete cap to provide the building's footprint. The structural steel would be erected on top of these caps. If the pilings had been laid end to end, they would have formed a line 31 miles long. The foundation work for the building was completed in about half the time originally projected. The job took only 48 days.

By January 1931, steel work was already well underway. (Cleveland Public Library collection)

Once the foundation was complete, structural steel and reinforcing concrete work got underway. The project used some 4,600 tons of structural steel, 500 tons of reinforcing steel, and 15,000 cubic yards of reinforcing concrete. A further 65 tons of aluminum was needed to form the upper cap of the building. As the structural skeleton was rising, Cleveland Builders Supply Company

began to bring in the 3,300,000 bricks that the Stadium's exterior and interior walls would require, and soon the outer skin of the building began to take shape.

Construction proceeded at a rapid pace, exceeding almost everyone's expectations. The warmest winter in a decade contributed to the speed with which the Stadium was rising. One wintery blast, however, brought tragedy to the site. On January 30, 1931, unusually blustery winds pummeled the site with sufficient force that they snapped the cables holding a scaffolding tower in place. Two workmen, Thomas Kelly and John Last, plunged 115 feet to their deaths when the tower gave way.

Construction crews completed their last day on the job on July 1, 1931, six months ahead of the projected schedule. The construction crews had completed the massive Cleveland Municipal Stadium in a remarkable 370 days. To help put that achievement into the proper perspective, one might compare it to the construction schedule for the Gateway stadium some 60 years later. The first concrete footers there were installed in April 1992, and the ballpark was finished in April 1994. Despite the "advantages" of modern construction equipment and techniques, the Gateway ballpark took nearly twice as long as the Stadium to complete.

(Above) The steel superstructure, its delicate look belying its structural strength, nears completion as winter wanes. (Osborn Engineering Company)

Construction was not without tragedy. Here, inspectors investigate scaffolding which collapsed, killing two steel workers, January 30, 1931. (Cleveland Press Collection of the Cleveland State University Archives)

When accountants tallied the final construction bills, the Stadium's price tag turned out to be $3,035,245, some 21% over budget, a frequent feature in publicly funded projects. Officials, however, sought to blunt criticism for the overrun by explaining that it had not been the cost of the Stadium itself, but rather the automobile and pedestrian bridges over the lakefront railroad tracks which resulted in the higher total. A decision to install field lighting, a scoreboard, and a sound system had also added to the cost. The City drew the extra funds from bridge construction bond sources and from an additional City Council appropriation. Again, to put the Stadium's construction deficit in perspective, the Gateway ballpark was originally projected to cost $132 million, but its final price tag was calculated at $171 million, a cost overrun of nearly 30%. Unlike the Stadium, whose overrun was covered by other immediately available funding sources, the total Gateway deficit of some $28 million (for arena, ballpark, and ancillary structures) took some two years and additional borrowing to resolve.

On July 2, 1931, the grand "lady by the lake" as future pundits would refer to her, was ready to greet her first patrons. The massive structure measured 800 feet in length and 720 in width. Its outer perimeter measured 2,640 feet. It stood 115 feet high, the equivalent of an eleven-story building. The building occupied 13.2 acres (considerably larger than the 9.4 acres of Public Square), and its playing field measured 4.2 acres.

In order to reduce the apparent mass of the building, Walker and Weeks had anchored the spectator oval (the building exterior actually formed a polygon rather than an oval) with four four-story towers. By shifting the upper deck's outer skin from

As brick work continues, installation begins on the roof in March 1931. (Cleveland Public Library collection)

brick to aluminum and recessing its placement, the architects sought to minimize the facility's vertical thrust.

When it opened, Cleveland Municipal Stadium was the largest in the world to feature individual rather than bleacher-style seating. The seats themselves varied in size. The most expensive seats, those closest to the field, were 20 inches wide. The reserved area seats were 19 inches, and the remainder were 18 inches. The Theodore Kundtz Company installed the seating.

The Stadium nears completion in April 1931. In the foreground, work has started on a pedestrian bridge to the Courthouse. (Cleveland Public Library collection)

Building on the Fast Track

The original permanent seating capacity of the Stadium was 78,189: 37,896 seats in 51 rows in the lower deck, 29,380 in 34 rows in the upper deck, and 10,913 in 52 rows in the bleachers. Planners estimated that for football games additional seating could be installed which would raise the total capacity to 90,000, and for an event such as a boxing match, which would permit field seating, the Stadium's seating capacity could be further increased to 110,000.

The Stadium's field was installed by the firm of Henry J. Babcox and Son. Workers laid the drainage tiles eight inches below the surface, and then covered them with topsoil. For the baseball infield, the company chose one part clay to two parts sandy loam, and the grass mixture was 60% Kentucky blue and 40% bent. The track surrounding the playing field was composed of cinders.

The late decision to add field lighting to the building cost the city $40,000. That investment resulted in 250 1,000-watt lamps ringing the field, attached just above the facing of the roof.

The Stadium had five entrances, one in each of the four perimeter towers and another in the bleacher section, with a total of 48 turnstiles. From the lower concourse, 42 portals led to the lower grandstand. Sixteen ramps took visitors to the top of the main grandstand, and another eight led from there to the upper deck. The

In spring 1931 access ways to the Stadium are in final stages of construction. (Cleveland Public Library collection)

upper concourse had 38 portals leading to the seating area. The Stadium provided a total of 48 lavatories, 38 refreshment stands, and 25 drinking fountains.

Thursday, July 2, was an inviting summer day, and the Stadium's silvery aluminum upper deck gleamed brightly, as Old Glory flew proudly from the flag pole. At noon the Stadium's doors opened for the first time, and Clevelanders were invited for free tours.

That evening at 8:00 the Stadium's formal dedication took place. The city fathers were expecting a crowd of some 75,000 for the festivities, but to their surprise only about 8,000 turned out for the event. Though the crowd was slim, it was not spared the expected celebratory rhetoric. Former City Manager William Hopkins was an honored guest, and he predicted that not only would the Stadium be "an enduring monument to the spirit and aspirations of our people but will take its place among the best known structures of the world." Current City Manager Morgan proclaimed that the "ancient world never saw a structure like this."

Then a 100-piece orchestra and 1,500-voice choir treated the attendees to the Stadium's first musical event. One of the numbers they performed was entitled "Stadium Song." It had been written for the occasion by Albert Cornsweet, City Manager Morgan's secretary.

The gleaming new addition to the lakefront is ready to begin a long career of civic service to the Greater Cleveland community. (Cleveland Public Library collection)

Fifty years before civic planners would again focus their thinking on the potential of the city's lakefront as a natural people attraction and seek to develop it accordingly, Cleveland Municipal Stadium had begun the process. Over the next 65 years, hundreds of millions would make their way to the lady by the lake to worship their God, honor their country, and cheer on their teams. A memorable chapter in the city's history had begun.

CHALLENGES AND CHANGES

3

While Greater Clevelanders may have looked at their mammoth new stadium with civic pride, city officials had to be more dispassionate. They had assured voters that revenue from the new facility would be more than sufficient to pay off its bonded indebtedness, a claim which opponents of the project had challenged. Right from the very beginning, however, the city's director of public property could see that keeping that commitment would be an uphill struggle.

Opening night at the Stadium revealed one of the problems which had not been adequately dealt with during construction. By locating the Stadium north of the lakefront railroad tracks, the City had taken advantage of available land, but the decision also situated the facility away from convenient public transportation. The nearest streetcar line ended in a loop near the pier at the bottom of East Ninth Street, leaving quite a walk to the nearest Stadium gates. Only two roadways, West Third and East Ninth streets, permitted vehicular access over the railroad tracks, but they were narrow and thus constricted traffic flow. Once north of the tracks, drivers would then have to search for parking, which was in short supply. Pedestrians had access to a third bridge, which crossed the railroad tracks from just behind the Cuyahoga County Courthouse. The situation was destined to cause a traffic nightmare, and so on opening night police chose safety over convenience, and banned vehicle access north of Lakeside Avenue. This left many patrons with a longer walk than they might have found agreeable.

The City of Cleveland did not have the funds to widen the bridges, add another pedestrian ramp, and provide additional parking areas. Bond proceeds issued to build the Stadium had been expended, and with the Great Depression deepening and human service needs increasing, the City was unable to tap its treasury to remedy the problems. Nor was the Stadium generating the revenues that its promoters had foreseen.

A major reason for this revenue shortfall was that the City and the Cleveland Indians Baseball Company had been unable to work out a mutually satisfactory lease. Therefore the City's anticipated revenue from three months of baseball crowds did not materialize. Many more months would pass before the lease negotiations were completed, and the Indians would not play their first game in the Stadium until the end of July 1932.

The arrival of the Indians, however, did not really resolve the financial issues. Outfielders complained about soggy field conditions. So at the end of the 1932

For two years, 1936-37, the Great Lakes Exposition brought vitality to the lakefront and lessened the Stadium's isolation. (Cleveland Public Library collection)

season, the field was excavated to find the cause. The experts decided that the drainage system was buried too deep, and they also found that many of the drainage tiles had been crushed by rolling the turf. As a result the entire field had to be dug up, so that a new drainage system could be installed. New sod was laid just in time for the 1933 baseball season. Some expenses just could not be avoided.

Even after the Indians' officials had inked the lease, it would not be until ten years later, in 1942, that the Stadium would show an operating profit. That year operations netted the Stadium account $8,692. In actuality, however, this did not represent an overall profit. The City was obligated to approximately $125,000 a year in debt service on the Stadium bonds, so even with the modest profit, the City still had to find more than $116,000 to keep from defaulting on the bonds. In fact, only once during the 40 years that the City operated it directly did the Stadium books show an overall profit. That came in 1948, the year the Indians set a major league attendance record on their way to the World Series championship. The profit that year, however, was a rather laughable $1.00. Such financial realities meant that improvements to the Stadium or its surroundings would have to wait.

The Avenue of the Presidents was one of two Great Lakes Exposition features which survived the fair's two-year stay on the lakefront. (Cleveland Public Library collection)

Nearly seven million visited the lakefront during the exhibition's stay. A popular feature of the fairgrounds was the Donald Gray Gardens, immediately north of the Stadium. (Cleveland Public Library collection)

In 1933 Chicago hosted a Century of Progress exhibition on its lakefront, and Cleveland leaders closely monitored the venture. They were looking for an appropriate way to celebrate the centennial of Cleveland's incorporation as a city in 1936. The Chicago experience was a marked success, and so Cleveland's civic leaders decided to sponsor a fair of their own.

Cleveland business leaders agreed to sponsor the Great Lakes Exposition, as it was called, and they chipped in $1.5 million to make it happen. The Exposition was situated on some 135 acres, occupying the Mall and the vacant lakefront land from the Stadium east to East 20th Street. A wooden "Bridge of the Presidents" connected the lakefront exhibits to those on the Mall. The exposition's grounds were attractively laid out; appealing but temporary exhibit buildings dotted the fair site. The Exposition opened on June 28, 1936, and ran for two summers, during which approximately seven million people made their way to the lakefront to enjoy its offerings. It closed on September 15, 1937.

Broken windows and a pile of debris mark the aftermath of a 1936 explosion blamed on a leaking gas line. (Cleveland Press photo, Jim Toman collection)

Not long after the close of the first summer's Exposition events, Cleveland Stadium was rocked by an explosion. The detonation was powerful; it shattered windows, cracked the concrete in three sections of the grandstand, and ripped out some 500 seats. Investigators at first thought that a bomb had gone off, but inspectors on the scene traced the cause to a frayed electrical wire which had sparked gas from a leaking line. Because the Exposition was closed for the season and

Although the explosion in 1936 caused much internal damage to the Stadium's structure, fortunately it occurred after the facility was closed; no one was injured. (Cleveland *Press* Collection of the Cleveland State University Archives)

the Stadium was empty at the time, no one was injured in the mishap. Repairs to the facility cost the city $18,000.

Only two remnants of the Great Lakes Exposition survived the show's 1937 closing. One was the Bridge of the Presidents. The temporary structure remained in service for both pedestrians and taxicabs until 1940. Afterward, it was restricted to pedestrian use only, and in that service it survived until 1949.

The other remnant to survive the Exposition's departure was the Donald Gray Gardens. Sponsored by the Garden Club of Cleveland, the gardens were named in honor of the man who had designed them, the popular garden editor of the Cleveland *Press*. Built on newly filled land directly north of the Stadium, the terraced gardens sported thousands of annuals and numerous varieties of trees, shrubs, and rosebushes. A line of pillars marked the gardens' northern boundary with the Stadium, and sloping walkways connected the Stadium to the floral displays below.

Built right to the edge of Lake Erie, the gardens were constantly threatened by erosion. Then in 1946 the City announced plans for Erieside Avenue which would circle north of the Gardens on newly reclaimed land and connect East Ninth with West Third streets. That decision saved the gardens, but a lack of adequate maintenance by the ever financially strapped City allowed them to deteriorate. Periodically attempts were made to improve the gardens, but without ongoing care, they could not retain their original beauty. The Donald Gray Gardens and the row of pillars marking their border with the Stadium outlived the rest of the Great Lakes Exposition by 59 years. They survived until December 1996 when bulldozers made short work of them. Their acres were needed for construction of the new football stadium.

In 1938 construction began on the 8,000-foot long Main Avenue Bridge, which would connect the east side and west side portions of the new Shoreway along the lakefront. Existing buildings forced the bridge north and over the railroad tracks as it passed the Stadium. One casualty of the highway construction was the pedestrian walkway connecting the Courthouse to the Stadium grounds. That was a loss for pedestrians, but west side drivers gained more direct access to the Stadium. Exits at Lakeside Avenue and East Ninth Street eased their approach to the facility. At about the same time, on October 3, 1938, the Cleveland Railway Company abandoned its streetcar service to the East Ninth Street Pier. The loss of the streetcar line, which had only operated during the summer months, made the Stadium even less accessible to people who chose not to drive there.

The Donald Gray Gardens, although losing their original luster over time, survived until the Stadium's demolition in December 1996. (Cleveland Public Library collection)

Major league baseball introduced night games in 1935. In Cleveland, however, the 250 field lights which had been installed in the Stadium in 1931 were not adequate for the demands of baseball, and so in 1939 the City replaced the original fixtures with more powerful ones. Just six years later, in 1945, the City undertook a complete revamping of the field lighting system. Six lighting towers, bearing 716 lamps, 1,500 watts each, were installed on the roof. In 1948 another 80 lamps were added.

Following World War II, the newly founded Cleveland Browns decided to make the Stadium their home, and in 1947 the Cleveland Indians made the Stadium their full-time venue. As the use of the Stadium increased, the City realized that it would have to do something to improve access. Since the 1938 loss of the pedestrian walkway behind the Courthouse, the only connection between West Third and East Ninth streets to the Stadium had been the dilapidated wooden bridge left from the Great Lakes Exposition. A source of ongoing public complaint and in decrepit condition, the old walkway was finally replaced by a modern one in 1949.

In 1950 the City again reached into its coffers to the tune of $350,000. Electrical engineers again improved the field lighting. This time the number of rooftop lamps increased to 1,318, nearly doubling the intensity of the 1945-1948 installation. The City also built a new ticket office for the Indians at Gate A, and it installed two auxiliary scoreboards on the facing of the upper grandstand.

In 1953 the main scoreboard was rewired, while still retaining its original external appearance. In 1961 the board's inner workings underwent further modification, but this time its exterior was given a more modern look. New scoreboard equipment allowed it to sound trumpet fanfares, flare fiery gas jets, shoot off fireworks, and print fan messages. The changes were due. The modern sports fan had come to expect more for the price of his or her admission.

Some Stadium visitors had complained that the area around the building was inadequately lighted, and so new exterior and perimeter lighting was added in 1959. In 1960 the City installed a new press box for football writers. The press box

The area around Cleveland Stadium was constantly changing over the years as landfill operations continued. Top photo shows the area in the mid-1940s, bottom photo in the 1960s. (The Cleveland Press Collection of the Cleveland State University Archives)

stretched from sections 7-9, and was situated where the very top rows of seats in the upper grandstand had been located. While the new facility improved the working environment for the scribes, there was chronic complaining about the number of steps they had to climb to reach it. Additional roof boxes were also installed at this time, giving broadcasters and coaches an unobstructed view of the field. Access to the roof boxes was through the football press box.

In 1962, the Cleveland Indians installed a giant Chief Wahoo, the team mascot, at roof level near Gate D. The illuminated and rotating sign reminded passers-by that the Stadium was home to the Tribe. (Following the 1993 season, the Indians' last at Cleveland Stadium, the sign was taken down and restored. It now is on display at the Western Reserve Historical Society in University Circle.)

Since the football writers had received a new press box, the City did not dare ignore those covering the baseball beat. In 1962 a pressroom, dubbed the Wigwam, was opened in Tower A, and in 1965 a new field press box, accommodating 110 writers and broadcasters and stretching from sections 19-25, was installed overlooking home plate. The new press facility cost $200,000.

By this time the Stadium was nearly 35 years old. While the city had provided some modest improvements, the facility was clearly showing its age. That

The football press box was opened in 1960. The facility also served as the Skyview Terrace for private parties during baseball season. (Jack Muslovski photo)

was particularly true when Clevelanders compared it with the new stadiums springing up around the country to accommodate the expansion of Major League Baseball and the National Football League.

In 1965, former Cleveland Indian third baseman Al Rosen spearheaded a campaign to rehabilitate the lakefront ballpark which many visitors felt was looking dingy. Rosen organized Group 66 to lobby the City for funds to make some major changes. Well supported by the media, Group 66 succeeded in bringing its agenda before Cleveland City Council, and in December 1966 Council authorized $3,375,000 in bonds to finance a major renovation project.

Both the Indians and the Browns, whose corporate offices were located in Stadium Towers A and B respectively, were cramped for space. Additions, faced in matching yellow brick, were grafted onto both towers, increasing office work space and providing patrons with new ticket centers. Work crews also cleaned the rest of the Stadium's outer brick wall at this time, removing a 35-year accumulation of grime, and restoring its original light yellow surface.

The plans also called for some interior improvements. A total of 1,100 new box seats were installed in the lower deck, bringing the lower box seats closer to the field of play. Unfortunately, the closest seats were positioned too low, and the seats behind them were insufficiently sloped, resulting in less than satisfactory sight lines for the house's premium seating. To accommodate the new seat placement, the baseball dugouts were also lowered, resulting in a less favorable view of the field for players and coaches as well.

To improve access to the upper grandstand, two escalators were installed, one between gates A and B, and the other near Gate D. The moving stairways significantly reduced the strain for patrons who sometimes found the Stadium's long ramps daunting.

The fourth floor of Gate A was also expanded and renovated. Indians' president Vernon Stouffer used his restaurant expertise to convert the space into a

A new baseball press box was added in 1965. Six sections long, the press box could accommodate 110 writers and broadcasters. (Jack Muslovski photo)

Stadium Club for Indians' season ticket holders. The Club offered full dining services during ballgames and provided patrons with closed-circuit access to the action on the field. Unfortunately, the club did not attract the volume of business that had been anticipated, and so the space was later remodeled and reopened as a restaurant for the general public.

The City also installed new field lighting as part of the Group 66 package. New lighting technology had made the 1950 installation obsolete. A total of 920 of the older lamps were replaced by modern halide fixtures, while 398 of the incandescent lamps were retained. The new lighting was equivalent to 54,857 standard 100-watt bulbs, a number sufficient to provide a community the size of Shaker Heights with adequate home illumination.

Cleveland Municipal Light (now Cleveland Public Power) provided the Stadium's electrical power. It delivered the power at 11,500 volts, which Stadium transformers converted into 2,300 volts before feeding it to the rooftop lighting towers. Because night time lighting at the Stadium required so much power, Stadium engineers were instructed to call the utility first before turning on the lights; otherwise the surge in demand could have caused brownouts or other system outages. The relighting project was widely hailed in the industry, and at the time it made the Stadium one of the four best-lighted facilities in the country.

The Group 66 improvements to the Stadium cost the City almost as much as it had spent on the original construction. Despite the expenditure, the Stadium was still in need of further updating. The City, however, was not in a position to finance them.

Cleveland had reached its population and employment peak in 1950, but two decades later, the city was reeling. It had lost a quarter of its population, dozens of industrial plants stood idle as jobs fled to the suburbs or to the South, and the central city still bore the fresh scars of two civil disturbances arising from the twin scourges of poverty and racism.

Regionalization of city facilities became the chief means for keeping up with infrastructure needs. It spread the costs to the wealthier and more populous suburbs. The parks, the port, the sewers, and the transit system were all turned over to county or regional agencies. Despite this reapportionment of infrastructure responsibility, the City still did not have any money available to make further improvements in the Stadium. At the same time, Stadium operations were running more than $300,000 in deficits annually. In March 1970 Cleveland City Council President James Stanton suggested that the only way that further improvements could be made at the Stadium was for the facility to be leased to private enterprise. He suggested turning it over to the Indians and the Browns to operate. At the time both Browns' owner Arthur B. Modell and Indians' President Vernon Stouffer had been sending up trial balloons about replacing the Stadium with a new facility.

In 1968 Stouffer had tried to rally public support for a new domed stadium. He managed to convince city, county, and state officials to invest $120,000 for a study of what was needed to create an ideal new sports facility. Charles Luckman and Associates of New York City carried out the conceptual work. Luckman's report called for a domed building with a seating capacity of 56,000. He projected that it could be built for about $49 million. If the capacity were to be increased to 65,000 seats, the price tag would escalate to over $60 million. At the time of the report,

This was a 1968 rendering by Luckman and Associates of a new stadium for Cleveland. Nothing came of the plan. (Cleveland *Press* Collection of the Cleveland State University Archives)

however, none of the governmental entities, and certainly not Stouffer nor the Indians, were in a position to finance such a dream facility. The plan was mothballed.

A couple years later, the Popil plan was unveiled. It called for constructing a dome over Cleveland Municipal Stadium at an estimated cost of $44 million. Not all engineers agreed with the projections. Some said that not all of the engineering requirements had been fully studied. Others said that the job would undoubtedly cost more. These objections, however, probably did not make any difference. There was simply no public money in sight to invest on athletic facilities.

Responding to Council President Stanton's idea for private management of the Stadium, three potential operators came forward. One was Sheldon Guren, president of U.S. Realty Investments, owner of the Terminal Tower. Another came from Christopher and Associates, which suggested improvements not only to the Stadium itself, but also building a hotel adjacent to it. Osborn Engineering, which had designed the Stadium, also offered a plan for total redevelopment of the Stadium area.

A fourth plan, and the one which ultimately was accepted by the City, came from Browns' owner Art Modell. Modell had ideas for renovating the Stadium, and he formed Cleveland Stadium Corporation to negotiate with the City the complex issues involved.

The Popil plan would have covered Cleveland Stadium with a retractable dome; thus reconfigured, it would seat 74,000. (Cleveland *Press* Collection of the Cleveland State University Archives)

At about the same time, the Cleveland Indians changed ownership, and Nick Mileti took over the helm of the baseball club. Unlike his predecessor, however, Mileti's main attention was not focused on the aging Stadium his baseball team played in. He was more concerned about the too small Arena on Euclid Avenue that his basketball and hockey clubs called home. He had determined to find them a new facility, and he was looking to Richfield, Ohio, for a site where he could build it.

This left Art Modell the only one still interested in assuming responsibility for the Stadium. Through his Stadium Corporation, Modell began discussions with the City of Cleveland in 1972, but the pace of negotiations proved very slow. Frustrated over the situation, Modell then began to consider that he too might have to look to the suburbs for a new Browns' facility, and in 1973 he purchased 200 acres of land in Strongsville, where he thought he might construct an 81,000-seat stadium for his football team.

The pressure from seeing its indoor sports teams moving to the Coliseum in Richfield and the imminent danger of losing the Browns to the suburbs prompted the City to give priority to settling the Stadium issue. After a year-and-a-half of negotiations, the two parties finally reached agreement for a 25-year lease of the Stadium. The lease was signed on October 10, 1973.

The lease was long, and its terms were complicated, but in general it provided for three things. First, Cleveland Stadium Corporation would operate the facility and receive all operating income while paying all operating costs. In return, the corporation agreed to spend $10 million on improvements to the Stadium within the first ten years of the contract. Lastly, the City would benefit from admission and property tax payments, as well as from rentals paid by Stadium Corporation. The agreement essentially took the City off the hook.

As for Modell's company, it took on considerable risk, but it also put itself in a position to make the improvements the fans were demanding and to sponsor other events which would help pay off the Corporation's investment. Stadium improvements, by making the venue more attractive to patrons, also seemed likely to benefit the baseball and football tenants, and thus assure that they would keep their franchises in Cleveland. The lease, therefore, appeared to set up a win-win situation. It was to run to the end of 1998.

Stadium Corporation assumed control of the facility in 1974. The most dramatic of the changes the new landlord had planned for the Stadium was the construction of 108 bi-level loge boxes, 84 of which would seat ten patrons, and 24 to accommodate eight. The loges were suspended from the bottom of the upper deck and ran the entire length of the Stadium, except for the area occupied by the baseball press box. The installation cost $3.6 million and was completed in time for the 1975

The most expensive and dramatic change in the Stadium came in 1974, when work began on installing 108 bi-level loges. (Cleveland Stadium Corporation photo, Jim Toman collection)

Challenges and Changes

baseball season. The ten-seat loges originally were leased for $15,000 per year, and the eight-seat variety for $10,500. The price included admission to all home baseball and football games, reserved parking, and cleaning and maintenance services.

The loges offered heating and air-conditioning, as well as both indoor and outdoor seating. Furnishings included a refrigerator, sink, coffee maker, and a television wired for the Stadium's closed-circuit broadcasts. Each loge also had storage space and a private lavatory.

The loges were very popular with Cleveland businesses and were totally leased from 1975 through 1993, by which time yearly lease prices had escalated to $59,000 for the larger units and $45,000 for the smaller ones. Starting in 1991, however, those prices also included tickets to all special events held at the Stadium. Only after the Indians left the Stadium for Gateway in 1994 did vacancies occur. That year prices were reduced to $55,000-$49,000 for the larger suites, depending on location, and to $39,000 for the smaller ones. Despite the lowered prices, competition from the two Gateway facilities for loge rentals resulted in major vacancies occurring for the first time at the Stadium. In 1994, only 72 suites were rented, and in 1995 only 78.

Another major undertaking was the lowering of the playing field. Because the 1967 renovation had caused problems with the sight lines from the lower box seats, the Cleveland Indians had asked that the field height be adjusted to correct the condition. Following the end of the 1975 football season, the field was excavated and lowered 30 inches, and 10,000 feet of new drainage tile was installed. Since officials of both the baseball and football teams preferred natural grass, a new surface of Merien Blue grass was planted.

Challenges and Changes

Each bi-level loge provided kitchen, lavatory, television, and storage amenities. (Jack Muslovski photo)

When installing the new field, the arrangement of its crown was changed. In the earlier field, the crown was near second base, and the field sloped downward toward the bleachers. In the 1975 reinstallation the field was given a four-inch crown along the home plate-second base axis, the slope towards left and right fields. The new arrangement took some getting used to by the ball players. Charley Johnson of the St. Louis Cardinals complained about it; he told Browns' officials that in the past whenever his team had won the toss, it would choose to play the last quarter, when the players were most tired, facing the goal in the bleacher end. That was downhill traveling. The new crown took away that kind of field advantage.

The new field was also less than trouble free. After the 1976 football campaign, the field was again torn up and another 15,000 feet of drainage tile installed. Five years later an additional 2,700 feet were added. Drainage tiles were located two, four, and eight inches below the playing surface.

Cleveland Stadium's field faced some severe tests. It was one of the few natural grass venues which hosted both baseball and football teams, the others being San Francisco, Atlanta, and Anaheim. Cleveland, however, had to contend with winter conditions that these other cities were spared. On top of the strain that the two sports put on the field, even greater problems were caused by the thousands of rock concert fans that danced on the field. The movement of these large crowds led to greater compaction of the soil, which in turn led to drainage problems.

In order to get the field to look its best for baseball, new sod was installed almost every spring. The practice was successful aesthetically, but new grass failed to develop the root system that would develop over several growing seasons. In general, the field needed major work every three years. At these intervals, the crown would be rebuilt, and the composition of the field reconfigured into just the right combination of sand and clay to minimize accumulative compaction. The pitcher's mound (which was all clay) would also be rebuilt, and the track would get a new topping of crushed red brick. The less compacted field brought about immediate, if temporary, improvements to drainage efficiency.

The Stadium's history saw very few groundskeepers. Three generations of the Emil Bossard family cared for the field between 1935 and 1983. David Frey was head groundskeeper 1983 to 1993, and Vince Patterozzi in 1994-1995.

Besides the loges and field work, as part of its improvement package, Stadium Corporation also installed a new scoreboard. At the time it was the largest single matrix screen in any sports facility. Measuring 86 by 29 feet, the board

Challenges and Changes

required 23,000 lamps. Work on the new board began after the last football game in December 1977, and the new board was ready for operation by the start of the baseball season in 1978. To operate the new board, a computerized control room was built into the baseball press box area. The project cost $1.5 million.

Other improvements made by Stadium Corporation were also welcomed by the fans. The food and beverage areas were modernized, and in 1981 a new elevator, between gates A and D, was installed. The elevator provided better access for people with disabilities, and situated at the end of the football press box, it also eased the climb (and the complaints) of the writers and coaches who used the box and the rooftop facilities. Less noticeable, but just as important, new wiring and plumbing throughout the building brought the facility into compliance with modern building code requirements. These improvements cost another $4 million. By 1982, one year ahead of schedule, Stadium Corporation had satisfied its lease commitment to spend $10 million in capital improvements.

Near the Stadium other welcome changes were also taking place. In 1973 both the City of Cleveland and Cuyahoga County began construction on new parking garages. The county's Huntington Park Garage, with 1,100 spaces, was erected behind the Courthouse, and the city's Willard Park Garage, with 1,500 spaces, went up behind City Hall. During construction the pedestrian bridge from Mall C was closed, creating a temporary inconvenience for Stadium patrons. In 1977 the bridge reopened, and both new garages provided easy access to it. Automobile access to the Stadium had been improved.

By the end of 1983 Cleveland Stadium Corporation had been responsible for the Stadium for ten years. It had spent more than $10 million on the old building in major refurbishing projects, and daily maintenance was significantly improved over the years when the City had taken care of the facility. The Stadium looked brighter, cleaner, and more modern.

Overhead, though, clouds were forming. And while they did not then appear ominous to Stadium watchers, they spelled increasing problems for the long-term health of the venerable sports palace. While further improvements to the Stadium would be made, obstacles to its survival as the city's foremost athletic facility began to mount.

Cleveland Stadium's entire surface was dug up in 1975 to provide better drainage; at the same time, the field was lowered to achieve improved sight lines from the box seats. (Cleveland Stadium Corporation photo, Jim Toman collection)

TIME RUNS OUT

Although Cleveland Stadium Corporation had made considerable improvements to the aging lady by the lake, some voices in the community continued to lobby for a new facility. Chronic complaints about how cold it could be on the lakefront to watch baseball in April or football in December fostered the belief that Cleveland should have a domed facility. There were other complaints about the Stadium, too. Many had to do with the columns that supported the upper deck and the roof. The columns partially blocked the views of the playing field for some 44,805 patrons whose seats were located behind them.

In 1982, Herb Kamm, editor of the Cleveland *Press*, counseled the community that it was time to invest in a new Stadium. The importance of a new facility became clearer in 1983 when Gabe Paul, president of the Cleveland Indians, then in negotiations with Cleveland Stadium Corporation, filed lawsuits against the Stadium landlord, demanding a larger share of concessions income. Implicit in Paul's suits was that the baseball franchise could move to another city if Cleveland could not offer it the conditions necessary to operate successfully.

The sturdy look of the Cleveland Browns' sign above Gate E that greeted Stadium goers belied the fragility of both the franchise and the facility. (Cleveland Press Collection of the Cleveland State University Archives)

In light of the Indians' complaints, Cleveland Mayor George Voinovich and *Plain Dealer* publisher Thomas Vail joined in the call for a new stadium. These developments created enough momentum that soon the community began to hear of plans for a domed stadium to be shared by the baseball and football teams. Officials of both the Indians and the Browns endorsed the concept.

On February 13, 1984, county commissioners Vincent Campanella, Virgil Brown, and Timothy Hagan voted to place on the May ballot a 30-year bond issue for construction of a domed sports complex. Preliminary plans called for a facility that would seat 70,000 and which could be built for about $150 million. The bonds would be supported by an increase in the property tax.

Many objections were raised to the method of financing. Governor Richard Celeste was among the most vocal opponents of using property taxes to fund the dome. His disapproval was apparently shared by most voters, and when they went to the polls in May, they soundly thrashed the idea by a margin of 277,845 to 147,221. The governor, however, was clear in stating that he favored a new stadium for downtown, and that he would work diligently to secure a sound basis for its financing.

In November 1984 a new Domed Stadium Committee was formed to prepare the way for a second attempt to secure voter approval. This time the committee's approach was to be more cautious, and it determined to develop a complete plan before returning to the ballot. The Domed Stadium Committee began its work by looking for a site for the new facility. Another Cleveland group, the Waterfront Steering Committee, had cautioned that a stadium was "not compatible for what we want to see on the lakefront." As a result of that pressure, the Dome committee eventually settled on the acreage surrounding the old Central Market, between Huron Road, Ontario Street, East Ninth Street, and Carnegie Avenue, as the home for the Dome project. With seed money from the State of Ohio and some bank loans, early in 1985 the Dome Committee began the laborious process of buying land there.

Just as planning moved forward for a new stadium, so too did developments on the lakefront. In 1985 the City of Cleveland unveiled its concept for what was then known as the Inner Harbor development. Essentially, the idea was to carve a huge basin into the area which was then the eastern end of the Stadium parking lot. The basin would be surrounded by walkways and landscaping, and eventually by a variety of museums. Modeled after what Baltimore had done with its waterfront, the idea was to make Cleveland's lakefront more people friendly and eventually turn it into a tourist attraction.

The parking lot was under long-term lease to the Stadium Corporation, but in the interests of aiding the city's waterfront planning, Stadium Corporation agreed to surrender most of the lot to the City in return for parking rights on

One of the blows to the Stadium's continued survival was to be the loss of the extensive parking lot to the east of the facility. (G.E. Company photo, Jim Toman collection)

Cleveland-Cuyahoga County Port Authority property to the west of the Stadium. Despite the exchange, almost 1,200 parking spaces were lost to Stadium patrons, leaving 9,345 spaces in the Stadium lots and in those adjoining Stadium property.

Excavation for the waterfront redevelopment began in 1986. To accommodate the location of the new basin, Erieside Avenue had to be relocated from the end of East Ninth Street. Its new layout gave the roadway a question-mark shape; it started from East Ninth Street south of the Stadium, then hooked around to the northern side of the Stadium before meeting up with West Third Street at its western end. Its relocation cost more parking places. The North Coast Harbor, as it was renamed in 1987, was formally dedicated on August 9, 1988.

During this period, Stadium Corporation officials continued to do their best to keep the Stadium a first-class facility, but they also wondered what the future held in store for the building. Though the Domed Stadium issue had been soundly defeated at the polls, a resolute effort was being made to pump new life into the project. At the same time, the City seemed to have plans for the lakefront which did not include Cleveland Municipal Stadium.

The development of the North Coast Harbor signaled new life for Cleveland's lakefront but spelled trouble for the future of Municipal Stadium. The Great Lakes Science Center (foreground) and Rock 'n' Roll Hall of Fame and Museum (background) occupied what used the be the main Stadium parking lot. (Greg Deegan photo)

Besides appropriating much of the Stadium's parking area for the Inner Harbor project, another indication that the City was not committed to the Stadium's future came in 1987. Attempts by various groups to have the U.S. Department of the Interior's National Park Service designate Cleveland Municipal Stadium as a national landmark were strenuously opposed by City of Cleveland officials. Such a designation would have made it very difficult for the City later to raze the building. So instead of naming the ballpark a landmark, the National Park Service on November 13, 1987, included it on the National Register of Historic Places, a category which recognized its historic importance, but which did not give it the protected status that a landmark designation would have conferred.

In the meantime Stadium Corporation officials were facing additional spending needs on the aging facility. In 1986 new roof boxes were installed, and

Though the Stadium's future remained in question, Cleveland Stadium Corporation continued to make improvements. The Stadium Restaurant, originally opened in 1967, was renovated in 1988. (Jack Muslovski photo)

in 1988 the Stadium Restaurant was remodeled. But at the same time another and costlier problem had arisen. The 1978 scoreboard was beginning to operate erratically as a result of industrial pollutants having affected its delicate electronic components. Experts recommended that it be replaced. Stadium officials also wanted to renovate the Stadium's lavatory facilities and enlarge and improve the home and visiting team locker rooms. Consultants were called in, and it was determined that a state-of-the-art scoreboard with video playback capabilities and with new television monitors ringing the lower grandstand and the main concourse would cost some $7.5 million. Restroom and locker room modernization would tack on another $2.5 million in costs.

At this point Art Modell and his Stadium Corporation staff realized that the only way that such improvements could be financed would be by extending the existing lease from 1998 to 2008. Since a new ballpark at the Central Market site was by no means a certainty, and since the Cleveland Indians were not then signed to a long-term lease, Stadium Corporation officials felt that further investment at the Stadium would stabilize the situation. Not only would it improve the venue for patrons, but also provide the baseball team with greater incentive to make a long-term commitment to remain in the city.

Accordingly Stadium Corporation officials on September 1, 1987, submitted their proposal to the City of Cleveland for a ten-year extension of the existing lease in return for Stadium Corporation's commitment to invest another $10 million in improvements.

For reasons that are still not clearly known, the City never held public hearings on the proposal, nor did it ever take any formal action regarding it. Perhaps the city fathers feared that permitting further improvements in the "old" Stadium would disincline voters to support a tax issue for a new one. Perhaps they did not want to wait until 2008 to proceed with plans for the makeover of the lakefront. Whatever the reason, for 15 months the Stadium Corporation's proposal sat in City Hall without action. Finally, in February 1989, disgusted by the delay, Art Modell withdrew the offer.

In 1989 the Stadium received its fourth – and final–scoreboard. The control room for the $4 million board was located in the baseball press box. (Greg Deegan photo)

Despite the setback with the negotiations, Stadium Corporation officials had a backup plan to do something about the malfunctioning scoreboard. They examined the budget to determine just how much could be spent on further improvements within the framework of the existing lease. The company decided to go ahead with a new board—minus the video replay capacity—and also to install 47 television monitors in the lower grandstand and along the main concourse. With 25,344 lamps, the new board cost $4.07 million; it was ready for the 1989 baseball season. At the same time the company decided to spend another $500,000 to refurbish the loges, which were showing the effects of 15 years of wear and tear as well as of exposure to the elements. The loges were repainted, recarpeted, and their furniture was reupholstered. They also received new televisions and microwaves. Four restrooms, those nearest gates A and B, were also completely renovated. These additional improvements raised the total capital investment of Stadium Corporation since the start of its operations in 1974 to $17 million.

Even as progress toward Stadium improvements was being limited by City of Cleveland inaction, just the opposite was happening on the domed stadium front. F. J. (Steve) O'Neill, owner of the Indians, had died in 1983, and trustees for his estate were trying to find a buyer for the team, one who would keep the Indians in Cleveland. As potential buyers came forward, their wish to operate from a baseball-only stadium for the team became a sticking point in negotiations. Finally, though, in December 1986, a successful sale took place. Local developers Richard and David Jacobs bought the team. In time the brothers made it clear that they too favored playing in a park designed exclusively for baseball. By 1987 the Central Market project was being redefined as an open-air park, seating about 42,000, and designed for baseball.

Though planning was moving towards accommodating baseball in a new facility, funding for such a project was not yet assured. This reality brought Art Modell and the Stadium Corporation back into the planning picture. Even though the City had not officially responded to his request for a lease extension, in spring 1989 he returned to Mayor George Voinovich with an idea for a major overhaul of Cleveland Stadium, one that would make the facility much more comfortable for fans and which would seek to meet the needs of both the baseball and football tenants. Modell committed Cleveland Stadium Corporation to spending $50,000 on a feasibility study by Ronald Labinski and the Hellmuth Obata Kassenbaum (HOK) firm. Osborn Engineering was another participant in the study.

In August 1989, however, the Indians seemed to throw cold water on the renovation idea when they publicly announced that they favored construction of a $150 million, 44,000-seat stadium on the Central Market site (by then known as Gateway, since the project would provide downtown with a new southerly gateway).

A model illustrates the Labinski plan for a renovated Cleveland Stadium—without columns or roof, but with a new bleacher section. The plan was first presented to the City of Cleveland in 1989, but the city took no action on it. (Cleveland Stadium Corporation, Jim Toman collection)

As a concession to Browns' fans, the baseball park would be designed in such a way that it could be expanded for football.

Art Modell, in turn, made it clear that the Browns were not interested in playing in a facility, which, even when expanded, would have fewer seats than the Stadium. A further sticking point was that more than 20,000 of the seats would be of the "temporary bleacher" variety, a condition that Browns' fans were unlikely to find acceptable.

Undeterred, therefore, by the Indians' announcement, Modell two weeks later held a press conference of his own at the Stadium. During the conference, which neither the mayor nor any representative from his office attended, Modell unveiled the Labinski-HOK model for a renovated Cleveland Stadium. The needs of Cleveland Stadium did not seem a priority to the City. It was apparent that the baseball and football teams were pulling in opposite directions.

By just about anyone's standards, Cleveland Stadium came up short in offering contemporary patrons the amenities that a new complex could provide. The Stadium's restrooms were located too far apart, and they lacked an adequate number of fixtures; this was particularly true for women. Its concourses were narrow, approximately only one third the width of those in new buildings. It offered only about half the number of concession stands and one tenth the water fountains that new venues provided. And while the Stadium did offer loges, it lacked premium (club) seating. The teams were also shortchanged. Locker room facilities were less than half the size of those in the new-age stadiums.

In the Labinski-HOK model, the Stadium took on a modern look. The roof would be removed, thus eliminating the need for columns in the upper deck. All seating in the lower grandstand behind the column line would be removed, and that area would be converted into a broad concourse with an ample number of concession stands and restrooms. To replace the seats lost from the lower grandstand, the field would be lowered about six feet and new seating would be added, sloping down to the field from the existing seating area. This design would create a virtually unobstructed view of the field from all seats. The existing bleacher area would be torn down and rebuilt as a two-story structure with new seating. Inside would be new team locker rooms, offices, and support facilities. All existing seats would be replaced with modern molded plastic ones. Thus updated, Cleveland Stadium would be comparable in design and amenities to most new stadiums. The renovated building could seat 72,000, and initial estimates suggested that the project could be completed for about $90 million.

Two competing stadium ideas were on the table. Clearly, the City was not in a financial position to consider both at the same time, so it would have to choose between the two.

Gateway won out. Packaged as a redevelopment issue, Gateway would consist of a new outdoor home for the Indians, an arena to bring the Cavaliers' basketball team back downtown, parking garages, and a plaza. The financing package was also settled. The project would be funded by a 15-year "sin-tax" on tobacco and alcohol products, as well as by revenues from leasing loges and club seating and by selling naming rights to the new facilities. Supporters of the Gateway issue claimed that it would spur additional private investment in the surrounding downtown area in the range of $344 million. Backers promised that all this redevelopment would create some 20,000 new jobs.

The Gateway issue went before the voters on May 8, 1990, and it came away with a narrow victory, 197,044 to 185,209. Still needed to complete the financing arrangements were final lease agreements with the Cavaliers and the Indians. When these were finally secured in December 1991, the project was able to move forward. Groundbreaking for the Gateway project, carrying an estimated $425 million price tag, took place in April 1992.

While the Indians were looking forward to playing in their new home, Stadium Corporation officials were wondering how to meet the facility's debt repayment schedule once its summertime tenant left the lakefront. Art Modell made it clear that he expected the City to compensate Stadium Corporation for the loss of

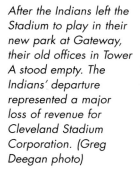

After the Indians left the Stadium to play in their new park at Gateway, their old offices in Tower A stood empty. The Indians' departure represented a major loss of revenue for Cleveland Stadium Corporation. (Greg Deegan photo)

the baseball team, and also that he expected that the Cleveland Browns would receive equitable treatment when it came to giving them a new (or like-new) home.

In the meantime, Cleveland Stadium had reached its sixtieth birthday, and it continued to require more than everyday maintenance to keep it operating efficiently and safely. In February 1990, Stadium Corporation had to replace the electrical transformers in the complex; the old ones had used PCBs, a substance no longer permitted by Environmental Protection Agency regulations. The replacement cost $365,000.

More vexing to Stadium Corporation was the 1990 requirement by Major League Baseball that field lighting again needed improvement in order to maintain player safety standards. The job was estimated to cost $375,000. What troubled Stadium Corporation executives, however, was the fact that by 1994 the Indians would likely no longer be playing at the Stadium, and that the existing lighting was more than adequate for football and other Stadium presentations. Nonetheless, the job needed to be done, and so contractors improved the field lighting in time for the 1990 season.

By 1994 the situation for Cleveland Stadium was looking bleak. For the first time since 1932 no baseball would be played there. The City had not come forward to make up the lost revenues which the Indians' move to Gateway cost Stadium Corporation, and so everything depended on sponsoring enough outside events to cover the shortfall. Despite extensive efforts to book concerts and other summertime events, in 1994 Stadium income fell short of budget by some $100,000.

When the Stadium was built in 1931, its art deco touches testified to its modern design. By 1995, however, the Stadium was considered obsolete by the NFL brain trust. (Jim Toman photo)

Gateway was negatively impacting Stadium revenues in another way as well. Faced with a decision about leasing a loge, companies now had three options to choose from: the new arena, the ballpark at Gateway, and Cleveland Municipal Stadium. Many were either unable or unwilling to lease loges at all three venues, and the lure of the new facilities (and perhaps some disenchantment with the football team) resulted in 24 unleased suites at the Stadium.

The Browns were also facing increasing amounts of red ink. The advent of unrestricted free agency in 1993 led to soaring player payrolls. As the financial problems facing the twin enterprises run by Art Modell escalated, the City of Cleveland finally began serious deliberations about the future of Cleveland Stadium. With Gateway finished, but by no means paid for, in summer 1994 City officials finally had at least the time (if not the money) to consider the needs of the Browns and the Stadium. Discussions between the two parties, however, did not proceed swiftly or smoothly. By 1994 the price tag for renovating Cleveland Stadium had escalated to $134 million, and the City had made it clear that it was expecting the Browns to make a $20 million contribution towards the budget. The Browns, however, were not in a position to advance any money at all. The team was deeply in debt and had reached its borrowing limit with the banks.

In December 1994 Modell commented about the protracted negotiations, that "If it can't be done and the public wishes that it not be done, I have to review my options." Cleveland Mayor Michael White then appointed a blue-ribbon Cleveland Stadium Task Force, David Hoag chairperson, to recommend how the Stadium issue could be resolved. The mayor quipped, "I don't want to wake up with a Baltimore hangover" (referring to Baltimore's having lost the Colts in 1984). Eleven months later the irony of his remark would be obvious.

The first decision the committee had to reach was whether the City should build a new football stadium or renovate the old one. That part of the puzzle was

Like its Stadium neighbor, the shadows were falling on the classical walkway of the Donald Gray Gardens, another remnant of Cleveland's 1930's progressive vision. (Greg Deegan photo)

soon answered. On January 26, 1995, the committee announced that it favored renovation. The decision was based solely on economic realities. A new stadium would cost the city about $220 million, whereas renovating the 64-year-old veteran was then estimated to carry a more modest $130 million price tag.

Perhaps to create a more positive community reaction to the need for financing Stadium renovation, stories about the benefits of the lease between the City of Cleveland and Stadium Corporation began to be aired. After 22 years of bashing the lease, the media changed its tune and the lease's benefits were extolled. Documents revealed that over the course of the lease, Stadium Corporation had spent some $53.4 million to improve and/or maintain the facility. At the same time, the lease was appraised at having annually saved the City some $500,000, which it otherwise would have had to drain from its general fund. In addition to the

44

savings on operations, the City also received some $9.3 million in rental income and saved $833,796 dollars in real estate taxes.

Various ideas also were being advanced that could add to the Stadium's economic potential. One group called for adding a sports mart to the eastern end of the Stadium. The facility would be the equivalent of a full-time merchandise expo for athletic equipment manufacturers. Another suggestion called for adding a hotel and office building to the east of the Stadium. These new facilities would increase the revenue stream for the total Stadium property. Another group suggested that after renovation, the Stadium could become home to an annual season of dog racing, thus providing added gate attractions to the too few that a football season and the periodic rock concert would generate.

While these ideas may or may not have had future merit, they did not represent an immediate source for financing the renovation commitment. The Task Force, therefore, began tackling the difficult riddle of where to find the funds for the renovation. The Gateway complex was complete, but it was millions of dollars in debt. Cuyahoga County was plagued by the loss of some $115 million in its SAFE investment program. And even as the committee searched for a funding solution, the task became more troubling. As engineers studied the Stadium's needs more thoroughly, the cost for the renovation kept increasing. In May 1995 the cost was fixed at $154 million, and one month later, with utility relocation costs figured in, it jumped to $172 million.

Art Modell must have sensed that he could not hold on financially much longer, nor could he see how the cash-strapped City and county would be able to come to the rescue. On June 5, 1995, he declared a moratorium on further discussions about the Stadium's future. Some Greater Clevelanders assumed that the moratorium was simply a bullying tactic by the Browns' owner to force action on the Stadium project. Others feared that its meaning was more ominous. With hindsight, it seems clear that by then Modell must already have reached the conclusion that he had to move his football team out of the city.

The moratorium notwithstanding, the Cleveland Stadium Task Force continued to hone its recommendations for funding the renovation. The committee suggested that Cleveland enact an 8% tax to be levied on off-street parking and a 2% increase in the admissions tax. That part of the funding package was approved by Cleveland City Council on June 29, 1995. Another piece in the funding pie was an extension of the sin tax which had been levied for Gateway, but that would have to wait for voter approval in the November election. The committee's plan also called for a $23 million contribution from the State of Ohio, $16 million from the private sector, and $10 million from the Browns.

Observers were not optimistic about the likelihood that Cuyahoga County voters would approve the extension of the sin tax on alcohol and tobacco products, and so backers launched a major campaign, featuring radio and television commercials and full-page newspaper ads. The ads called Cleveland Stadium "a symbol of our history and our town." The ad copy went on to state that the Stadium was the "site of some of the most exciting, memorable, and historic moments in our lives—from world championship games to world renowned musical events. Voting Yes will preserve these memories." Despite the intense campaign effort, a week before the election, the outcome appeared too close to call.

The weekend before the election, rumors began to circulate around town: The Browns were moving to Baltimore. Then on November 6, just one day before the vote, Art Modell confirmed those rumors from a rostrum in downtown Baltimore. Greater Clevelanders responded with shock and outrage. But more than that, they responded with their votes. They were not going to give Art Modell the excuse that there was no money to fix up the Browns' longtime home. One day after Modell's announcement, they went to the polls and gave the Stadium renovation issue the most overwhelming endorsement that any stadium issue had ever received. The issue passed with a whopping 74.4% affirmative vote, 256,278 "yes's" to 98,113 "no's." Once again Cleveland Municipal Stadium had become the focus of Greater Clevelanders' civic pride and commitment.

The victory at the polls was the Stadium's last triumph, and sadly the victory would prove to be pyrrhic. Despite the overwhelming endorsement of the community to save and refurbish the legend on the lake, a 64-year-old facility, even extensively renovated, would not provide sufficient economic incentive for the National Football League to guarantee Cleveland a replacement team.

By January 1996 a deal between the NFL, the City of Cleveland, and the Modell interests had been struck. Cleveland could keep its brown and orange team colors. It could retain the "Browns" name. It could keep the impressive records of its football achievements. And NFL tradition would return to the city in 1999. Cleveland Municipal Stadium, however, which the sin-tax campaign had identified as the key to preserving the memories of great moments, would become only a memory itself.

The Stadium, as the repository of those great memories, was sentenced to disappear from the lakefront. The next chapters, however, testify why the memories of the thrills it provided for 65 years will not soon be effaced.

A TRULY MULTI-PURPOSE PLACE

Over many years, Cleveland Municipal Stadium came to merit a certain distinction in terms of its size, versatility, and durability. The facility's real claim on the loyalty of Greater Clevelanders, however, was only marginally related to its structure and its improvements. More important than bricks and steel, the Stadium became a repository of memories. Whether those moments stemmed from the thrill of sport, the emotion of music, the chill of patriotism, or the conviction of religious faith depends on the person. Cleveland Municipal Stadium hosted them all and lived up to its original billing of being a truly multi-purpose facility for so many Clevelanders.

While most people associate the lakefront field with its two long-time tenants, the Cleveland Indians baseball team and the Cleveland Browns football club, the Stadium was never conceived exclusively as the home for professional sports. And, it did not operate that way. What the promoters promised the citizens in 1928—that the Stadium would be used for a wide variety of functions—was certainly the case during the facility's 65-year history. From the time it opened in 1931 until the wrecking ball crashed into its side and sealed its death, Cleveland Stadium's schedule was filled with diversity.

The Stadium's opening festivity included a civic night with a choral flavor, but the main event during that curtain-raising week was held on the second night, July 3, 1931. That evening the lakefront facility hosted the world heavyweight boxing championship between Max Schmeling and

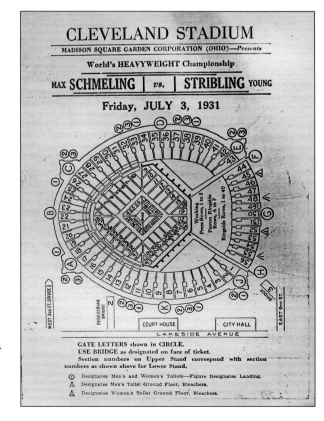

This was the program that greeted patrons to the first event (after the dedication ceremonies) to be held at Cleveland Stadium. (Osborn Engineering Company)

Temporary seating was used to bring patrons closer to the ring for the Stribling-Schmeling fight. Workers check to be sure all is ready for the event. (Cleveland Press Collection of the Cleveland State University Archives)

Young Stribling. Fight promoters, hoping the excitement of a new stadium would swell the crowd, immediately began to encourage fans to attend the event. Visions of outlandish profits must have engulfed them as they contemplated a possible crowd of 110,000, which was Stadium capacity if field seating was included.

Unfortunately for planners, the matchup between Schmeling, the defending champion from Germany, and Stribling failed to capture the public's imagination. The match was Schmeling's first defense of the title he had won from Jack Sharkey in New York City in 1930. A crowd of 36,936 (which included 6,006 passes) showed up to watch Schmeling successfully defend his title, winning by a TKO in the fifteenth round.

The next day, the Stadium hosted its first fireworks spectacular, an event which would become one of the most popular and crowd-pleasing of all Stadium attractions. Sponsored by the American Legion, the Independence Day celebration included a ballet pageant with 350 dancers and two 1,000-voice choruses in addition to the pyrotechnic grand finale. An audience of 16,506 attended.

Just two weeks later, the Stadium baseball field was inaugurated. Cleveland that week played host to the Shrine's national convention. Among the many activities of the week, the Shriners put on a colorful parade which culminated at the Stadium in a "Night in the Orient" pageant and the facility's first baseball game. A crowd of over 30,000 enjoyed the show and saw Al Koran Shrine defeat Al Sirat Grotto, 6-1.

Events in the following few weeks would give the new Municipal Stadium its first real test of versatility. While Cleveland's reputation for its commitment to and involvement in the fine arts had been well established, few would have expected the city's lakefront field to host a grand opera. Yet, it did. Sponsored by the Cleveland *Press*, the opera festival was held the week of July 28.

The stage, which measured 300 feet by 125 feet, was called the largest ever built for an operatic performance. Workers erected the stage across the baseball infield with its center point above second base. Because of the stage location, the

A Truly Multi-Purpose Place

Stadium was necessarily dressed; for the performances promoters offered seats in only 13 sections, which numbered about 20,000 seats. Ticket prices ranged from 25 cents to $3 for an upper deck box seat. The opening performance featured *Aida*, and a crowd of 18,063 was on hand. The next two evenings presented *Cavalleria Rusticana* along with acts from *Die Meistersinger* and *La Gioconda*; together these two performances brought out another 26,565. *Aida* returned on Friday for a house of 19,147, and again on the closing Sunday before 14,222. The Saturday feature, comprising parts of *Carmen*, *Die Meistersinger*, and *The Bartered Bride*, which showcased Cleveland's own Czech chorus, attracted 10,711 people. For the entire week, 88,708 were in attendance. Unfortunately, while the setting and stagecraft were impressive sights, the acoustics were disappointing. Thus, Opera Week marked both the first and last operatic performances in Cleveland Stadium.

A religious event on September 6, 1931, provided the first crowd to truly test the Stadium's capacity. That day, the Holy Name Society of the Roman Catholic Diocese of Cleveland rented Municipal Stadium for a prayer service. The occasion marked the tenth anniversary of Bishop Joseph Schrembs' installation as head of the diocese. Approximately 70,000 gathered that Sunday to pay tribute to their bishop. For the first time in the Stadium, the sounds of the throng were directed toward the realm above rather than to the field below.

Soon, though, many athletic events were scheduled for the Stadium field. Soccer made its debut on September 7, 1931, with the Cleveland Federation of Labor's celebration of Labor Day. As part of the festivities, a soccer match was held. Football's lakefront premiere came just two days later. The Cleveland Indians, an early city entry into the still struggling National Football League, played an exhibition game against a semi-pro team sponsored by Pennzoil. About 35,000 fans saw the fledgling Indians prevail, shutting out Pennzoil, 10-0. College football was next to appear. John Carroll University hosted the debut college event at the Stadium and played its entire 1931 season there. The Blue Streaks played Adrian College in their

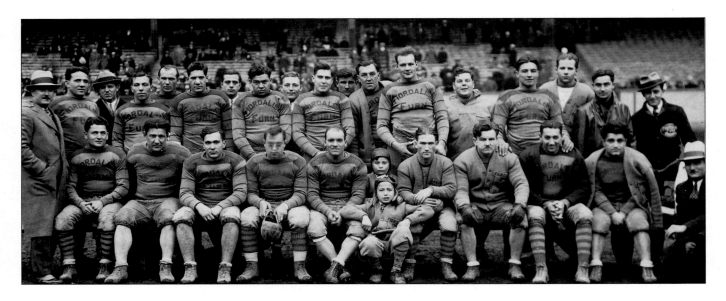

Amateur football had a regular presence at Municipal Stadium. The Fiordalisi Furniture team captured the city championship in 1931. (Mike Speranza collection)

first game, held on September 24, 1931. A sparse turnout of just over 2,000 people watched John Carroll prevail, 26-6. The university continued to make Municipal Stadium its home football field through the 1935 season, and until the early 1950s played there regularly. John Carroll holds the distinction of having held more contests at the Stadium than any other college.

The inaugural high school football game also took place in 1931. Cleveland East Tech battled Cleveland West Tech to a scoreless tie in front of approximately 8,500 fans. The contest, played on October 3, represented the first game ever to be played at night by a team from the Cleveland scholastic high school senate.

Beginning in the inaugural year of 1931, the Stadium hosted perhaps some of the most memorable high school football games in the area. It was decided that the Stadium would host the annual city football championship game between the winners of the East Senate and West Senate. That first year, the game featured a matchup between Cathedral Latin School and Central High School in front of 19,304 fans. Latin shut out Central, 18-0. That championship game was the first in a series at the Stadium which would continue until 1968. The annual contest, which in time became popularly known as the Charity Game, proved to be a favorite for Greater Clevelanders. Eleven times the games drew crowds of over 40,000; five games had more than 50,000. The largest crowd of 70,955 attended the 1946 game, which saw Cathedral Latin blast Holy Name High School, 35-6. For all the championship games, Benedictine High School holds the record for the most appearances (16).

Interest in the Charity Game, played around the Thanksgiving holiday, began to fade in the middle 1950s, but then seemed to catch a second wind in the early 1960s. Around this time, Benedictine and St. Ignatius high schools faced each other in three consecutive years. In 1968 heavy rains kept the crowd turnout minimal as only 17,582 saw St. Ignatius and John F. Kennedy High School play to a 14-14 tie.

Sponsors thought a change in format might be needed to reverse the trend, so in 1969 they scheduled a doubleheader. The crowd, though, did not measure up to hopes, as only 15,671 came through the turnstiles to watch Benedictine defeat St. Ignatius in the first game 18-7, and St. Joseph High School shut out St. Edward High School, 22-0. In 1970 sponsors tried one more doubleheader, but attendance did not even reach 11,000. Facing competition from televised professional football, complications from family holiday plans, and the unappealing November weather on the lakefront, the series' popularity had waned. After 1970, the City Championship game was resumed, but games were held elsewhere.

Another popular series held at Municipal Stadium was the football rivalry between the University of Notre Dame and the U.S. Naval Academy. The first contest on the lakefront field took place in 1932, with Notre Dame defeating Navy 12-0 before 61,554 fans. The second game, held in 1934, brought Navy revenge against the Fighting Irish, as the Midshipmen edged their rivals 10-6 before 57,124 spectators. Altogether the two teams met on Stadium turf eleven times (1932, 1934, 1939, 1942, 1943, 1945, 1947, 1950, 1952, 1976, and 1978). The series drew a total of 767,036 fans, an average of 69,730 per contest. The largest crowd came to the 1947 contest, when 84,090 watched the Irish shut out Navy, 27-0.

Over the years, other college football teams played at the Stadium as well. The lakefront field hosted teams from the former Case Institute of Technology and

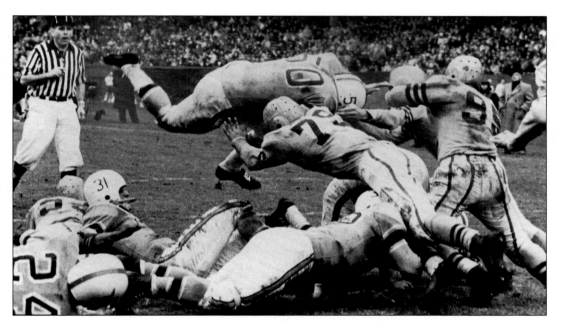

In this 1957 edition of the high school Charity Game, the Benedictine Bengals drubbed the St. Ignatius Wildcats, 27-3. Benedictine High School appeared in the annual classic more times than any other high school. (Cleveland Press Collection of the Cleveland State University Archives)

Western Reserve University (the schools merged into Case Western Reserve University in 1967). Municipal Stadium also held four Ohio State University games. OSU began the series in 1942 with a game against Illinois, handing the Illini a 44-20 shellacking before 68,656 fans. The next year the Buckeyes lost to the Purdue Boilermakers, 30-7, but the following year they beat the Illini again, 26-12. Illinois returned to the Stadium in 1959 for a game against Penn State, and Ohio State returned for the fourth time to play Northwestern in 1991. In that contest the Buckeyes defeated the Wildcats 34-3 in front of 61,221 fans. Other college games throughout the Stadium's history included the Great Lakes Academy, which played Pitt in 1942, and the College All-Stars game against the NFL's Cleveland Rams in 1941. On October 18, 1975, the Mid-America Conference presented a college football doubleheader featuring Western Michigan versus Toledo and Kent State versus Bowling Green. Kent

Ohio State's marching band performs its famous Script Ohio formation in Cleveland Stadium during halftime of the Buckeye's game against Northwestern in 1991. (Cleveland Stadium photo, Mike Poplar collection)

State returned to the Stadium in 1976 for a game against the Air Force Academy. Central State played Tennessee State in 1987.

The lakefront facility also hosted track and field events. On August 21, 1932, about 55,000 people made their way to the Stadium to watch athletes of that year's Olympic Games put on an exhibition. Clevelander Jesse Owens, the East Tech High School graduate, won the 100-yard dash in 9.6 seconds. He received a roaring standing ovation, the kind especially reserved for local champions. Leo Sexton also received much applause as that day he set a new record in the shotput.

Final staging details are being prepared for the Autumn Festival of 1933. Acrobatics and other circus stunts helped entertain the crowd. (Cleveland Press Collection of the Cleveland State University Archives)

Despite the fact that so many associate Municipal Stadium with sporting events, it was a religious festival that set the facility's all-time attendance mark. The Diocese of Cleveland in 1935 hosted the Seventh Eucharistic Congress of the Roman Catholic Church. The central purpose of the Congress was to strengthen devotion to the Eucharistic sacrament. With the full panoply with which Catholicism traditionally celebrated its rituals, and with the fervent participation of its adherents, downtown Cleveland became the center of a colorful and moving four-day series of religious events. It was estimated that during the Congress nearly half a million Catholics were in the city for the various services.

A Truly Multi-Purpose Place

The Stadium was an eerie site as 75,000 Catholic men held lighted tapers during a midnight Mass as part of the 1935 Eucharistic Congress. (Catholic Universe Bulletin)

Because of the number of people involved, original plans to use Cleveland's Public Auditorium had to be scrapped, and planners scheduled the main events for the Stadium. On September 24, about 75,000 attended a midnight Mass at the lakefront facility. At the consecration of the liturgy, the lights were extinguished and the only illumination in the shadowy park came from 75,000 lighted tapers held by the worshipers. Those attending commented that it was an awesome sight to see the cavernous Stadium aglow with candlelight.

The next day, a Sunday, the finale of the Congress drew a crowd of more than 300,000 onto the streets of downtown Cleveland for a procession in which the Eucharist was to be carried from the Cathedral of St. John the Evangelist, at East Ninth Street and Superior Avenue, to the Stadium. The colorful procession consisted of children in their school uniforms, groups of laymen in their organizational dress, the religious and priests of the diocese in full clerical garb, and most of the bishops of the United States in full episcopal regalia. Patrick Cardinal Hayes, Archbishop of New York, carried the monstrance, which held a large host for worshipers to view.

The largest throng in Cleveland Stadium history, 125,000, attended the closing ceremonies of the Eucharistic Congress. Here part of the crowd forms a "living monstrance" on the playing field. (Cleveland Press Collection of the Cleveland State University Archives)

It took three hours for the procession to wend its way to the Stadium. There every seat was filled. Thousands more stood at the rear of the grandstands. The field had been outlined by 100,000 flowers in the shape of a monstrance. Into that floral outline processed the 22,000 marchers. Altogether the crowd in the Stadium for the afternoon Benediction service numbered approximately 125,000. That total marked

the most people ever in the lakefront park at one time, and that number was never to be surpassed.

Of a much different variety was a Stadium twin bill in 1939. A crowd of 44,267 arrived at the Stadium for an unusual bit of programming. A Wild West Rodeo was to take place, followed by a Benny Goodman Swing Concert. For the rodeo, the field was strewn with the necessary props. There were ramps for motorcycle stunts, a brick wall through which a car was to hurtle, and wooden barricades which could be set on fire and through which cars would race. Corrals were erected to hold the animals, and performers tried bronco busting, calf roping, and stunt riding. Then the Goodman band took over, and the audience enjoyed a jitterbug jamboree followed by one of the band's classic swing concerts.

The first eleven July 4 Festival of Freedom celebrations were held at the Stadium. Here a packed house watches the 1946 edition. (Cleveland Press Collection of the Cleveland State University Archives)

As forces in Europe and Asia moved closer to a second World War, patriotic themes took on greater importance nationally and locally. In Cleveland, that spirit was exemplified in a Festival of Freedom, a tradition begun in 1939 and which continues today. The inaugural event was held at the Stadium on July 4, and it featured an orchestral tribute, a community sing-along, a parade of flags, a nationality pageant, and speeches by local politicians. A grand finale fireworks show culminated the program. A year later, with Europe reeling from war, the crowd of 75,000 got involved in the show. In a darkened Stadium, each person struck a match and held it high as a symbol for liberty.

With each passing year, the Festival of Freedom grew in popularity. Often, the Stadium would be crammed with 80,000-plus crowds, and outside thousands more would gather to watch the fireworks display. By 1950, the festival had outgrown the Stadium. That year, organizers moved the show to Lakefront Airport where a crowd of 200,000 assembled for the fireworks extravaganza. The airport allowed both more room for people and superior logistics for staging the fireworks show. In 1954, the festival moved once more, this time to Edgewater Park. That year the Cleveland Indians were engaged in an exciting pennant race and were scheduled to play a night game on the holiday. City officials, concerned that the crowds for the game and the festival would swamp the downtown area, decided to move the show west to the park. Ever since, Edgewater Park has been home for the annual Festival of Freedom show.

Other patriotic shows have taken place at the Stadium, too. In 1942, with the United States at war, the Cleveland *News* sponsored a boxing card at the Stadium, with the proceeds earmarked for "Bombers for MacArthur." The famous U.S. general was then planning his next advances toward the Philippines in an attempt to wipe out Japanese resistance in New Guinea. A crowd of 23,574 turned out for the boxing matches and to support the war effort.

Just a few weeks later, the Army Show came to town. On September 14, 1942, the lakefront looked like it was being invaded as 2,000 troops arrived in

The big guns of the Army Show deafened the large crowds which came to the Stadium in 1942 in support of the Emergency Relief Fund. (Cleveland *Press* Collection of the Cleveland State University Archives)

400 railcars and bivouacked in the area just east of East Ninth Street. The Army Show was designed to educate the public about the realities of war and to raise money for the Army Emergency Relief Fund. All week after their arrival, the troops converted the parking lots around the Stadium into a model "battle depot," a display of the machinery of war including guns, tanks, and even captured German and Japanese planes.

The city's three daily newspapers gave the Army Show much coverage, and broad interest was generated for a series of mock battles which would take place nightly at the Stadium beginning on Friday, September 18. Tickets for the benefit ranged from 55 cents to $2. A crowd of 36,732 attended the opening-night show. No sooner had they taken their seats than the air above the Stadium was filled with the roar of engines from a squadron of warplanes. It was the opening salvo in a 90-minute show.

Municipal Stadium's bleachers were reconfigured to look like a model fortified Japanese village. The village became the target of an all-out assault, featuring howitzers, mortars, machine guns, and aerial cannon. Volley after volley directed at the "enemy position" shook the Stadium with an overwhelming din that made the thunder of fireworks pale in comparison. After 90 minutes of mayhem, the flag of surrender was raised over the bleachers, and the U.S. Army and the crowd celebrated the victory.

Word of mouth carried the enthusiasm of that first night's audience. The attendance swelled to 54,432 for the second night, then to 63,201 on Sunday, and to 76,654 on Monday, before closing on Tuesday before a house of 60,601. In five days the Army Show drew 291,620, all of whom by their presence contributed to the war effort.

After the ending of World War II, the Stadium schedule featured more peaceful events. In 1946, the facility hosted another major religious event, this time

for the Jehovah's Witnesses, who held their district convention in Cleveland and wanted to use the Stadium for their chief gatherings. A throng of 80,000 filled the lakefront facility for the assembly. Some citizens noticed, though, that the U.S. flag was not flying during the meeting; they were offended because they thought the flag was not raised in deference to the Witnesses' conviction that the flag was a graven image prohibited by Biblical injunction. Investigation into the matter revealed that it had simply been an oversight by a Stadium worker. The assembly continued without further discord. Converts during the gathering were taken from Municipal Stadium to Edgewater Park,

The Jehovah's Witnesses used Cleveland Stadium twice for their assemblies. A packed house is on hand for the 1946 program. (Cleveland Press photo, Jim Toman collection)

where they were baptized in the waters of Lake Erie. The group returned to the lakefront facility again in 1975 for another district assembly. A total of over 213,000 attended the four days of their June gathering.

Another sport made its debut in the Stadium in 1947. Officials booked midget auto racing, which at the time was gaining popularity, on a trial basis into the Stadium schedule. A great deal of work, however, was needed to make the field suitable for midget racing. Workers had to remove ten feet of sod on the inner side of the track to provide for a thirty-foot racing strip. Then they had to install a rail fence, eighteen inches high, along the inner track line. The track's cinders had to be replaced with clay. These modifications cost the racing sponsor over $25,000.

The alterations to the field brought an immediate protest from the Cleveland Indians and from their groundskeeper, Emil Bossard. The ball club's complaint was that baseball and auto racing were incompatible. Team management expressed concern that the modifications to the field created conditions that were more likely to lead to injuries to the ballplayers. Despite the Indians' protests, Cleveland Mayor Thomas A. Burke approved the lease with the sponsors of the midget racing card.

The first race, held on June 14, 1947, featured leading figures from auto racing such as Mauri Rose, Al Bonnell, and Bill Holland. A crowd of 21,197 came for the inaugural event, and many of them were given a mudbath, as the autos quickly turned the newly laid track into a soggy mess. A second race took place the next weekend, and 16,565 attended that event. During the program, Bill Boyd, one of the drivers, was injured when his racer overturned. A third race was held on August 2. That event left the field in so deteriorated a condition that Burke was forced

A Truly Multi-Purpose Place

to act. Exercising his prerogative under the terms of the lease with the racing sponsors, the mayor vetoed any further use of the Stadium for auto racing.

More in keeping with the Stadium's basic purpose was an Outdoor Sports Show which held forth at the lakefront for ten days in September 1947. The main attraction of the show was a 102,000-gallon water tank installed in the baseball infield. The 40-by-100-foot pool was used for log-rolling and canoe-tipping contests. It also served as the stage for Sharkey the Seal, who amused the audience with his juggling skills. The sports expo also featured both a horse show and a dog show.

The 1947 Stadium schedule provides a good indication of just how busy the lakefront facility could be. It also serves an example of how varied the events were that the Stadium hosted. That year, the Stadium held 77 Cleveland Indians' games, seven Browns' games, three midget racing cards, a Festival of Freedom, a Veterans of Foreign Wars convention, the outdoor sports show, a model airplane racing contest, the 38th Annual Cleveland Baseball Federation Amateur Day, and three high school and two college football games.

There was one more important event held at the Stadium in 1947. Professional baseball at that time was still basically represented by racially segregated leagues. Although Jackie Robinson broke the racial barrier with the Brooklyn Dodgers that year, most black baseball players were still playing in the Negro major American and National baseball leagues. Over the years, Cleveland had been represented in the American Negro League by several different teams, beginning in 1922 when the Tate Stars held the city's banner. Beginning in 1943, Cleveland's eighth franchise, the Buckeyes of the American Negro League, began to show signs of challenging for the Negro World Series. In 1945, the Buckeyes won the World Series of the Negro

Leagues. In 1947 their achievements again led them into the series against the New York Cubans of the Negro National League. Municipal Stadium was the site of the second game in the series, but despite the Buckeyes' home field advantage, the Cubans prevailed, 6-0. The final game in the series was also scheduled for Cleveland, but it was played in League Park, where most of the Buckeye contests were fielded. The Buckeyes lost the game, 6-5, and with it New York captured the Negro League World Series.

The Stadium witnessed all levels of baseball. In addition to professional games, it also hosted amateur baseball, particularly the annual Cleveland Baseball Federation event, which raised money for local amateur teams. Throughout its long history, it was also the site for high school baseball, especially the Cleveland Senate championship games, and for college level games, including Cleveland State University's contests.

In 1950 Municipal Stadium became the stage for wild animals and aerial acrobatics as the Cole Bros. Circus entertained there for the first time. Cleveland had long been on the traveling show's circuit, but prior to 1950 its performances had been held first in the Public Auditorium, and then later under a big top in the Stadium parking lot. The three-day June visit had a top crowd of only 8,000, but the circus became a regular return attraction to the Stadium thereafter.

The summer of 1953 brought another interesting program bill. The Cleveland Orchestra, which annually produced a series of summer "pops concerts" held at Public Auditorium, agreed that year to schedule its concerts at the lakefront facility. To accommodate the orchestra, workers erected a special stage in front of the bleachers and installed a special sound amplification system. The concerts were scheduled to take place the same evenings as Cleveland Indians' baseball games. A rather bizarre feature of the arrangement was the timing of the concerts. The conductor was to lift his baton at the same time the Indians' batters were hefting their bats for pre-game batting practice. The inaugural event in this "doubleheader" series took place on

June 2. A crowd of 17,356 was on hand for the debut concert. The orchestra, led by conductor Louis Lane, played standard pop tunes, including a full orchestral rendering of "Take Me Out to the Ball Game." Surprisingly, music critics found the concert aesthetically satisfying, and baseball fans were just as pleased to see the Indians beat the Red Sox, 7-3.

A musical event of a somewhat different order was held at Municipal Stadium in 1966. It would become the first in what was to become a long series of similar events, establishing the lakefront field as a popular draw in music. On August 14, the British rock group, the Beatles, paid their second visit to Cleveland and their first to the Stadium. In their previous visit in 1964, over 100,000 Beatles' fans had clamored for tickets to their concert at Public Auditorium, a facility that could only accommodate about 10,000. The group's second visit, therefore, was planned for the Stadium to adequately address the anticipated demand.

Workers set up a stage at second base and they put up a fence around the infield. Unfortunately for tour promoters, a crowd of only 24,646 showed up for the superstar group. What the fans lacked in numbers, though, they made up for in enthusiasm as they trampled down the fence and surged onto the field to be nearer the stage. The concert had to be halted for 25 minutes until security forces could get the audience back to their seats. The reasons for the small turnout have never been fully explained, but the Cleveland situation, both in 1964 and 1966, mirrored that of other cities along the Beatles' tour trail.

In 1967, Vernon Stouffer and Gabe Paul, at that time executives of the Cleveland Indians, sponsored a Cleveland entry into the newly formed United Soccer Association. The Stokers, as the team was called, was imported from Stoke City, England, to serve as Cleveland's soccer representative during the summer season. The squad did rather well that first season, going 5-3-4 and finishing in second place. The Stokers played for Cleveland again the next year, this time in a consolidated North American Soccer League. They captured first place in their Lakes Division with a 14-7-11 record, and met the Atlanta Chiefs in playoff action at the Stadium on September 11. Before a dismal crowd of only 3,431, the Stokers battled the Chiefs to a 1-1 tie. Action then moved to Atlanta where the Stokers were eliminated from post-season play. Despite the team's on field success, it was plagued by poor attendance, a fact which inevitably doomed the franchise after the 1968 season.

One highlight from that 1968 season came on July 10 when the world-famous Pele came to Municipal Stadium to lead his team against the Stokers. A crowd of 16,205 came to watch the action and see Pele. The soccer star returned to the Stadium field in 1976 for a game between the New York Cosmos and the Dallas Tornado before a crowd of 14,119.

Baseball players listen as Louis Lane conducts the Cleveland Orchestra in a pops concert before the start of a 1953 Indians' game. The orchestra had to vacate its regular Public Auditorium home that summer while the facility was being renovated. (Musical Arts Association)

While other kinds of events and shows may seem to have dominated the Stadium schedule, the religious ones maintained a constant presence on Municipal Stadium's docket. One of the most successful and longest religious affairs took place July 14-23, 1972, when Evangelist Billy Graham brought his crusade to Cleveland. When the preacher first saw the lakefront facility, he expressed some concern that it might be too large for his purposes. But, by the time the crusade had concluded ten days later, he was very pleased that the organizers had chosen it as the site. A total of 372,440 turned out to attend the popular preacher's services, each enhanced by a huge choir. Ethel Waters was the featured soloist. More important to Graham, however, was another statistic. Of those who attended, 19,608 came forward to testify that they were willing to lead new lives for the Lord. The crusade provided a thought-provoking statistic for religious commentators and sports buffs alike. In just ten days, the crusade had garnered more attendance than had many sporting events in comparable periods of time.

Billy Graham's success in 1972 helped spur a return to the Stadium in 1994. The preacher proved his perennial appeal. During a five-day crusade from June 8-12, more than 250,000 trekked to the lakefront to hear his message. On one day alone, organizers held a "Teen's Crusade," which about 65,000 adolescents attended. The 1994 effort was the best turnout during a five-day North American crusade in the 50 years of Graham crusades. Municipal Stadium seemed particularly well-suited for events of a sacred nature.

There were other kinds of events as well. On June 16, 1984, motorized sport returned to the lakefront when a National Motor Spectacular was held. To prepare the facility for the tractor pull, 4,000 sheets of plywood had to be laid, and then 4,500 tons of dirt—15 dump trucks full—spread on top. While Cleveland Stadium Corporation officials expressed concern about the field, the event transpired without damage to the field. There were 24,512 in attendance. In 1987 the sound of revving

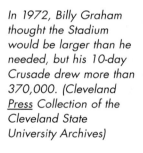

In 1972, Billy Graham thought the Stadium would be larger than he needed, but his 10-day Crusade drew more than 370,000. (Cleveland Press Collection of the Cleveland State University Archives)

A Truly Multi-Purpose Place

engines again filled the Stadium as TNT Motor Nationals came to town, attracting a crowd of 10,276. Again, there was no damage to the field.

The lakefront facility hosted many events of varied musical expression. In 1975 a polka festival was tried. Twenty bands, each with its own dance floor, were situated along the perimeter of the playing field. The weather did not cooperate, however, and only 1,602 attended. More successful was The World's Greatest Gospel Music Festival, held later that summer; it drew 9,390. Soul music was also represented at the Stadium. In 1983, the Cleveland Plum Festival featuring Aretha Franklin and Gladys Knight entertained a crowd of 26,763, and one year later, the Star Fest delighted 6,810. The Ohio Valley Jazz Festival called the Stadium home in both 1988 and 1989. These two-night events drew crowds of 32,530 and 14,160 respectively.

When the Cleveland Stadium Corporation assumed Stadium management in 1974, rock'n roll, absent since the Beatles' 1966 visit, returned to the lakefront in a major way. Under the sponsorship of Belkin Productions, Inc., the Stadium hosted a "World Series of Rock." On June 23, 1974, the opening event in the series was held. A combination attraction of Joe Walsh, Lynrd Skynrd, and the Beach Boys performed before an audience of 32,837. On August 4 a turnout of 34,173 came to hear Emerson, Lake & Palmer, and then on August 30, a crowd of 81,316 packed the Stadium to see and hear Crosby, Stills, Nash & Young.

The following year Municipal Stadium hosted four more rock concerts. The combined audiences who came to see Chicago and the Beach Boys, Rolling Stones, Yes, and Faces approached the 200,000 mark. In 1976, however, no concerts were scheduled; that year the field had been torn up and rebuilt. At the time, rock concert audiences were accommodated by laying a plywood surface over the field. Field specialists warned that the newly installed field would not be able to survive that kind of treatment without major damage. So, rock 'n roll took a hiatus from the lakefront in 1976.

In 1977 the rock beat resumed with three concerts. Aerosmith and Peter Frampton headlined two of the concerts, and Pink Floyd entertained a crowd of 82,986. That figure set a Stadium record for rock concert attendance, one that was never to be surpassed. The lakefront field scheduled and held four more rock concerts in 1978 and 1979– Rolling Stones, Electric Light Orchestra, Fleetwood Mac, and Aerosmith– but then an event occurred elsewhere which would profoundly impact the rock scene.

Concert goers often came in droves to the lakefront to watch their favorite musicians perform. Here, a sizeable crowd gathered outside Municipal Stadium in August 1977 hoping to seize the best seats in the house for a Peter Frampton concert. (Cleveland Press Collection of the Cleveland State University Archives)

In a Who concert in Cincinnati on December 3, 1979, 11 members of the audience were killed in a stampede when the crowd got out of control. Responding to the situation, the Ohio legislature, on the anniversary of the tragedy, handed the governor a bill which provided for tighter control of rock concerts. Among the restrictions was a cap on festival, or non-permanent, seating. Lawsuits in the Cincinnati case eventually resulted in over $2.1 million in damages. The heightened awareness of liability for crowd control and the specifics of the Ohio legislation meant that no crowd in the future would ever be able to top that of the Stadium's 1977 Pink Floyd concert. Capacity, in fact, would stand even less than available permanent seating, as stage location rendered some seats unusable.

Rock concerts at the Stadium resumed in 1982, and while their popularity remained unabated, attendance was affected by the new realities. The Michael Jackson concert, part of the much-anticipated 1984 Victory Tour, played the Stadium for two nights to a combined crowd of just over 81,000. The Jacksons played on the largest stage ever used at the time. The size of the stage, which measured seven stories high and stretched 159 feet wide and 91 feet deep, forced promoters to offer only 45,000 tickets for each show.

Hometown rock favorite Michael Stanley also performed a Stadium-related concert on September 29, 1984. To celebrate Cleveland's recent designation as an "All-American City," a free concert was held in the parking lot to the east of the lakefront facility. A crowd variously estimated at 60,000-75,000 attended and demonstrated their civic pride in a city making a comeback.

Bruce Springsteen held one of the most celebrated concerts at the Stadium on August 7, 1985. Because of his popularity during the time of his "Born in the U.S.A." tour, all the tickets for the performance were sold in three hours' time, a Cleveland record. His notoriety even impacted Municipal Stadium ushers, who were then in a labor dispute with management. The ushers agreed, in deference to Springsteen, to postpone any strike action until after the concert.

In the 1990s, Cleveland Stadium Corporation continued to recruit as many big-name rock acts to the lakefront. Genesis, Pink Floyd, the reunited Eagles, and the Rolling Stones, who came to the Stadium for their fourth time, all played before sizable crowds during the decade. Perhaps the biggest musical event to hit the Stadium since the World Series of Rock, however, was the concert for the opening of the Rock 'n Roll Hall of Fame and Museum, held on September 2, 1995. An estimated 60,000 fans were treated to a rock extravaganza, which featured many of the biggest names in rock history. Tickets ranged from $75 to $540 for premium seats. The show, which was performed on a double stage that included a revolving one built atop a wide, standard stage, lasted more than six hours and was aired nationally on HBO. Thirty-five bands and performers participated in 41 different musical combinations. Featured performers included Chuck Berry,

The largest crowd ever to watch a rock band in Cleveland Stadium— 82,896—enjoyed a show by Pink Floyd on June 25, 1977. (Cleveland Press Collection of the Cleveland State University Archives)

A Truly Multi-Purpose Place

Bruce Springsteen and the E Street Band, John Mellencamp, Martha Reeves, Bon Jovi, James Brown, Johnny Cash, Al Green, Little Richard, Bob Dylan, The Allman Brothers Band, Jerry Lee Lewis, The Kinks, Aretha Franklin, and Lou Reed.

Rock music had a long history at Municipal Stadium. Cleveland's claim as the home of rock'n roll was in part substantiated by the crowds and the enthusiasm with which Clevelanders embraced the Stadium rock concerts. It was fitting, then, that the lady by the lake would host one of the greatest popular musical events ever. The Concert for the Rock 'n Roll Hall of Fame and Museum was to be the last, but perhaps the most impressive, rock concert the Stadium ever hosted, a fitting tribute to the Stadium's role in popular music and to the city of Cleveland's enthusiasm for it. In all,

35 rock concerts took place at the Stadium, and almost two million fans came to the lakefront to enjoy the shows.

Bob Seger entertains a throng of almost 50,000 in a 1980 concert at the Stadium. (Cleveland Press Collection of the Cleveland State University Archives)

Faced with the loss of the Indians as tenants after 1993, Cleveland Stadium Corporation officials tried to generate some income by scheduling other sources of entertainment. Besides the Billy Graham crusade and the rock concerts, the 1994 schedule included a World Cup-bound U.S.A. soccer team which played Bayern, Munich, the club champions of Germany, in front of more than 14,892 fans on May 21. Unfortunately for fans of the U.S. team, Bayern had a 3-2 comeback victory against the American team. That summer, the Stadium also hosted a Monster Truck Jam and a Stadiumfest, which was a carnival complete with rides and other amusements. Dismal crowd sizes for these resulted in major losses for their promoters. The following year, the only two featured events were a May 20 Supercross, which drew 15,419, and the Concert for the Rock Hall.

After the fate of Cleveland Stadium was sealed, the City held one last hurrah. A weekend of farewell festivities, appropriately dubbed "The Final Play," was scheduled for September 21-22, 1996. As a last send-off to Clevelanders, officials dressed up the Stadium to host the final special event in its storied history. Vendors' booths ringed the playing field, and football attractions occupied center court. Huge banners depicting all the NFL teams' colors and logos (except for the Baltimore Ravens) were hung from the upper deck.

The Stadium field became the site for a Monster Truck Jam in 1994, one of the events that Cleveland Stadium Corporation used to fill the schedule void left by the loss of the Indians. (Cleveland Stadium Corporation Collection)

About 100,000 people attended "The Final Play," a last chance to take in the aura of the Stadium and walk on the field where legends were made. (Greg Deegan photo)

On the walls inside the Stadium, fans who attended "The Final Play" left final farewells to the lady by the lake, a touching reminder of what she meant to them. (Greg Deegan photo)

The weekend was an opportunity for the fans who had made the Stadium such a special place to take in the aura and relive their own memories of the legend on the lake. Fans responded overwhelmingly. They quickly snatched up 100,000 free tickets and came to the lakefront in steady droves even though the weather was grim and the field had turned into a mudbowl. Fans were welcome to roam the field, the concourse, and the Dawg Pound. They were able to participate in various activities such as kicking field goals, diving into the endzone, running races, and completing passes; these were put on by the "NFL Experience" traveling road show. Vendor booths offered memorabilia and autographs of famous Browns' players. A big screen television was erected near the Dawg pound on which Browns' highlights were played continuously. Some fans came adorned in brown and orange, others in Cleveland Indians' garb. Many were overheard reminiscing about memorable moments they had experienced.

Fans who had come to the lakefront for so many events and on such numerous occasions were able to say goodbye to the venerable facility, and they did so with heartfelt enthusiasm. On the yellow bricks along the ramps separating the bleachers from the rest of the Stadium, many scribbled their names. Some wrote messages such as "Thanks for the memories," "So long, Babe," and "Rest in peace, old girl." It seemed a fitting farewell.

On September 24 and 25, the last pieces of the Stadium were auctioned off. The scoreboard went quickly, as did the flag that flew over the lakefront facility for every Browns' contest. All kinds of bits of the Stadium, from toilets to players' lockers to vending equipment, were purchased by people, most of whom sought to keep a tangible part of Municipal Stadium as a complement to their many memories. When the final visitor left that day, the Stadium's gates closed for the last time.

To chronicle every event held at Municipal Stadium during its lifetime would not be practical. The lakefront facility hosted many and varied events and performers. It would be a rare Clevelander who does not cherish some special memory emanating from the Stadium. Throughout its 65-year history, its original billing as being a multi-purpose facility was evident by the yearly schedule of events. Yet, as interesting as those many events were, the Stadium was first and foremost the home of the Cleveland Indians and the Cleveland Browns. Their stories come next.

ROCK CONCERTS AT CLEVELAND STADIUM

ARTIST	DATE OF PERFORMANCE	ATTENDANCE
The Beatles	August 14, 1966	24,646
Joe Walsh Lynrd Skynrd Beach Boys	June 23, 1974	32,837
Emerson, Lake & Palmer	August 8, 1974	34,173
Crosby, Stills, Nash & Young	August 30, 1974	81,316
Chicago The Beach Boys	May 31, 1975	26,035
The Rolling Stones	June 14, 1975	78,665
Yes	July 11, 1975	29,394
Faces	August 23, 1975	61,512
Aerosmith	June 5, 1977	33,049
Pink Floyd	June 25, 1977	82,986
Peter Frampton	August 6, 1977	77,674
The Rolling Stones	July 1, 1978	82,238
Electric Light Orchestra	July 15, 1978	60,214
Fleetwood Mac	August 26, 1978	74,892
Aerosmith	July 28, 1979	65,807
Bob Seger	July 19, 1980	47,183
Michael Stanley (in parking lot)	September 29, 1984	est. 70,000
Michael Jackson	October 19-20, 1984	34,210 and 47,186
Bruce Springsteen	August 7, 1985	71,808
Pink Floyd	September 16-17, 1987	60,172 and 62,001
U2	October 6, 1987	50,456
The Who	July 19, 1989	61,120
The Rolling Stones	September 27, 1989	61,727
Paul McCartney	July 20, 1990	66,197
Genesis	May 25, 1992	49,877
Pink Floyd	May 26-27, 1994	53,311 and 46,963
The Eagles	July 8, 1994	45,432
The Rolling Stones	August 28, 1994	35,265
Concert for the Rock and Roll Hall of Fame and Museum	September 2, 1995	est. 60,000

NOTE: In addition to these concert events, both the Indians and the Browns sponsored occasional post-game concerts, including such performers as The Beach Boys, Crosby, Stills & Nash, Joe Walsh, Ronnie Milsap, and Aretha Franklin.

As Gateway was rising in the
foreground, Cleveland Stadium
was fading into the background.
(David Kachinko photo)

The Terminal Tower and Cleveland Municipal Stadium were Cleveland landmarks for 65 years. (Mort Tucker photo, Cleveland Stadium Corporation collection)

For Clevelanders, the Stadium was not just a place of sports thrills; it was also a place which could evoke civic pride and a spirit of patriotism. (Mort Tucker photo, Cleveland Stadium Corporation collection)

The yellow brick of Cleveland Stadium was a warm contrast to the blue of Lake Erie. (Cleveland Stadium Corporation photo, Jim Toman collection)

The sun was setting on the Stadium, and only 25 seconds remained on the clock as the Browns played their last game at the lakefront park, December 17, 1995. (David Kachinko photo)

The old landmark on the lakefront is dwarfed by the city's newest, Key Tower (right foreground). The Justice Center is to the left. (David Kachinko photo)

Cleveland Stadium was sold out
for the Indians' final three-game
series. The last game got
underway on October 3, 1993.
(David Kachinko photo)

Fireworks frequently rose over Cleveland Stadium as the sun set over Lake Erie. (James Spring photo)

A packed Dawg Pound was a Cleveland football tradition. (David Kachinko photo)

In its final year of operation, Cleveland Stadium shared the lakefront with the then in-progress Great Lakes Science Center and the Rock and Roll Hall of Fame and Museum. (David Kachinko photo)

On "Light-up Cleveland" nights when Monday Night football was in town, the Stadium was the brightest place of all. (Mort Tucker photo, Cleveland Stadium Corporation photo)

Crowds grew during the final season the Indians called the Stadium home—a Yankees' game in August 1993. (David Kachinko photo)

(Below) Cleveland Stadium's field became a carnival midway for the 1994 Stadiumfest. (Cleveland Stadium Corporation photo, Jim Toman collection)

(Above) Hollywood came to Cleveland Municipal Stadium for this 1991 filming of _The Babe Ruth Story._ (Paul Tepley photo, Cleveland Stadium Corporation collection)

(Left) The night sky over Cleveland Stadium frequently came alive with post-game fireworks. (Cleveland Stadium Corporation photo, Jim Toman collection)

By December 15, 1996, exactly
one year after the last football
game was played at Cleveland
Municipal Stadium, the once
seemingly indestructible landmark
on the lakefront was falling to the
wreckers' tools. (David Kachinko
photo)

THE CLEVELAND INDIANS
MEMORIES OF HOPE, MEMORIES OF DESPAIR

Many today associate the Cleveland Indians with their new, state-of-the-art ballpark, Jacobs Field. Yet, the story of the Tribe long predates the field at the corner of East Ninth St. and Carnegie Ave. In fact, Cleveland Municipal Stadium witnessed 61 years of Indians' moments and helped to define the baseball team as a foremost part of major league baseball history.

The lakefront field itself, though, was not the original home of Cleveland's professional baseball team. By the time the Indians played their first game at Municipal Stadium on July 31, 1932, the organization had already called five previous baseball fields home. The reason was simple. Professional baseball had its origins in Cleveland long before any stadium existed.

The Cleveland Forest City's had formed around the time that Robert E. Lee was signing the Confederacy's death warrant at Appomattox Court House in Virginia. An amateur team, the Forest City's organized in 1865 and played teams from other Ohio towns and cities. It was not until 1869, however, that the Forest City's became a professional team (the top player received $65 a month), having followed the lead of the first established professional baseball team, the Cincinnati Red Stockings. The Forest City's made their debut on June 2 of that year against the Red Stockings at Case Commons, which was located on East 38th Street between Scovill and Central avenues. Fans watching the game were only able to do so from field level, for there were no grandstands. Those fans that could get a clear view of the action, however, were probably quite disappointed. The Cleveland team was handily trounced by the Queen City visitors, 25-6.

The team moved east to its second home only two years after its introduction into the professional ranks. This time, the Forest City's called home a field at East

Fans at Cleveland stadium on July 31, 1932, for the first Indians' game at the year-old park, set a new major league attendance record. The absence of an outfield fence in the early years there made the Stadium a "pitcher's park." (Cleveland Press Collection of the Cleveland State University Archives)

League Park, situated at the corner of East 66th Street and Lexington Avenue, was the home to Cleveland professional baseball teams for 55 years. (Cleveland *Press* Collection of the Cleveland State University Archives)

55th Street and Central Avenue. The organization tried league play in the fledgling National Association, but it was not able to sustain itself financially and folded following the 1872 season. It was then not until 1879 that professional baseball resumed in Cleveland, this time under the nickname Spiders, so-called because many players were lanky and long-limbed. The Spiders, playing in the then-National League, held their games on a field between Cedar and Carnegie avenues near East 46th Street. The team remained there for five years until 1884, when the club went out of business.

Clevelanders were then denied professional baseball until 1887 when a reformed Spiders team joined the new American Association. The team had a new owner and new ballpark. Frank DeHaas Robison, the new owner, established a home field for the Spiders at the junction of Payne Avenue and East 39th Street. It was not coincidental that Robison owned the Payne Avenue streetcar line. In 1889 his team rejoined the National League but continued to play at East 39th Street until 1891, when Robison established a new stadium at East 66th Street and Lexington Avenue. The park, called National League Park, was designed by Charles S. Schneider, and was situated at the intersection of two other streetcar lines which Robison owned. In less than 25 years, Cleveland professional baseball teams had moved home fields four times. When Robison opened National League Park, however, professional baseball in Cleveland had found a home for the next 55 years.

The turn of the century witnessed a pivotal juncture in Cleveland baseball history. Following that year's baseball season, the owners of the baseball team dropped out of the National League. Charles W. Somers bought the team soon afterward, and in 1900 established it as one of the founding members of the

American League. The newly formed league began play in 1901, and with the new league came a new name for the ballpark. The "National" was dropped, and the ball field's name was shortened to League Park.

In the same year, the organization decided to change the nickname of the team as well. Actually, the moniker for the professional baseball team would change three times in the next three years. In 1901, they were called the Blues (or Bluebirds) because of the color of their uniforms (actually they were the old uniforms of the Spiders). Seeking a more macho image for the team, Somers altered the name to Broncos in 1902, but it was a name which the players did not like. So, in 1903 the owner asked area newspapers to run a contest to select a new name for the team. The winning entry was the "Naps," so called to honor the team's star second-baseman, Napoleon Lajoie, who had come to Cleveland the year before from Connie Mack's Philadelphia club. The Frenchman, who later became a Hall-of-Famer, and Addie Joss, a young pitching sensation whose career was to be cut short due to meningitis, led the Naps through the first decade of the 20th century. The highlight for the Naps came late in the 1908 season, when the team found itself in a pennant race with Chicago and Detroit. Despite Joss's 1-0 perfect game victory on October 2 against Chicago's Ed Walsh, the Naps finished in second place.

Cleveland's team remained the Naps until January 1915. Following a 1914 campaign in which the team dropped a record 102 games and drew just 185,997 paying customers, the team sold the aging Lajoie to Philadelphia. The last-place team was now without its star and its nickname, so Somers sought to give the club another moniker. He appointed sports writers from local newspapers to select a new name. The committee encouraged fans to suggest nicknames for the ball club, and soon, fans responded with many colorful names. One fan, making fun of the team's Nap-less status, suggested they be called the "Scraps," because, he wrote, "that's all that's left of 'em." Other names included Hustlers (submitted by a fan who thought the name would wake the team from the "Nap" which it was in the previous season), Grays, Tip Tops, Buckeyes, and Lakedgers.

Ultimately, though, the name that the committee chose was the Indians, one of the names of an old National League club which had played for a short time in Cleveland in the 19th century. With the announcement, *The Plain Dealer* joked, "The nickname, however, is but temporarily bestowed, as the club may so conduct itself during the present season as to earn some other cognomen which may be more appropriate."

League Park's composite right field wall was located only 240 feet from home plate. Almost every ball hit into right could be a game breaker. Games there were seldom dull. (Cleveland Public Library collection)

Although historians have referred to a contest in which the person with the winning submission selected the name to honor Louis Sockalexis, the first Native American to play in the major leagues, newspaper accounts of the time speak of no such contest. Instead, Somers' committee picked the nickname with fan input. When word got out about the new name for the team, many fans wrote letters approving the choice. Those who made their feelings known hoped the team's new identity would turn around its play, just as the Boston Braves had done in 1914 after receiving its "Native American" name. As Cleveland baseball history has shown, the name was anything but temporary. Despite recurring protests from those who feel the name is insensitive to the history of America's indigenous peoples, it has survived more than 82 years and seems likely to last even longer.

The stadium where the Indians played, however, soon received another new name. In 1916 James Dunn bought the team and facility from Somers for $500,000. He renamed the park Dunn Field, which it would be called until 1927, when the next owner, Alva Bradley, restored the field's name to League Park.

For the most part, League Park was a comfortable stadium. Expanded several times, it had a capacity of 27,000, which was large enough to handle the number of fans who attended most Indians' games, and its design brought fans close to the field of play. With its location at the intersection of two streetcar lines, it was also easy to get to. Perhaps best of all, the stadium's unusual field dimensions provided fans with many exciting plays. The left field line stretched 375 feet, and a home run hit to center field would have to sail an astounding 460 feet. The vast territory in center and left made fleet-footed and sure-handed outfielders a must. Right field in League Park, on the other hand, was a hitter's dream. The fence was only 240 feet from home plate, although it reached 40 feet in height. The bottom portion of the fence was made of concrete while the upper section was of wire. Any ball hit to right field had the chance to be a game-breaking hit, and the tall fence required fielders to be adept at playing the ricochet.

League Park did have its disadvantages. It could not adequately handle really big crowds, a factor that became apparent during the 1920 season in which the Indians won the World Series. During that year, attendance climbed almost 70 percent from the previous year. In addition, as the dawn of the automobile emerged, League Park's lack of adjacent parking became an increasing liability. The park was completely land-locked by neighborhood homes, streets, and trolley lines, and the absence of nearby parking made it a hassle for many fans to attend games. Constructing parking lots and expanding the stadium would have been a costly venture.

E.S. Barnard, who became club president on James Dunn's death, undertook to sell the Cleveland Indians for Dunn's widow. Barnard understood the limitations of League Park. For these reasons, he took a leading role in planning the lakefront stadium. Barnard fully expected the Indians to move their home from League Park to the Municipal Stadium. It came as something of a shock, then, when in 1931 Alva Bradley, the Indians' new owner, and the City of Cleveland were unable to reach terms for a lease at the new Stadium. Bradley's hesitation, however, was natural. At the time, the Indians would have been the only major league team that did not own the park in which it played. Bradley felt he had to protect the interests of the team, and so negotiations dragged on for months. It would not be until July 31, 1932, more than a year after the Stadium had been completed, that the Indians would play their first game at the lakefront park.

The Indians played the American League champion Philadelphia Athletics for the opening baseball game at the Stadium. The A's threw southpaw Lefty Grove, a future hall-of-famer, while the Tribe countered with Mel Harder, who would eventually post 223 wins for the team during his 20-year career. Actually Harder substituted for club ace Wesley Ferrell. Ferrell was in the midst of completing his fourth consecutive season winning 20 games, but he had been sidelined with a bad back. Cleveland fans, knowing the inaugural game would be an historic one, flocked to the lakefront. The crowd of 80,184 that sunny Sunday afternoon set a record for the most people ever to attend a baseball game. The Indians' organization provided the fanfare to fit the special occasion. Ohio Governor George White tossed the ceremonial first pitch to Cleveland Mayor Raymond T. Miller. Franchise officials also invited former stars to attend, including Lajoie, Tris Speaker, and Bill Wambsganss (two leaders on the 1920 world-champion Indians) and Cy Young, a former pitcher for the Cleveland Spiders of the National League during the last decade of the 19th century. Fans were not to be disappointed by the game. Although the Indians came up short, 1-0, they witnessed a magnificent pitching duel.

Unfortunately for the Indians, the opening game crowd was not a harbinger of things to come at the turnstiles. A major reason for the drop in attendance was that the Stadium opened during the heart of the Great Depression, and many Clevelanders could not afford baseball games. The 1932 attendance figure (468,953), for instance, was lower than the previous year by 3% percent, and was 13% lower than the 1929 attendance count (536,210). In 1933 the Indians played their entire home schedule at the Stadium, but attendance again dipped below the previous year's, and the number of fans attending baseball games was approximately 100,000 fewer than the team's last full season at League Park.

That 1933 campaign was not a successful one for the Indians. The hard-hitting team soon discovered that cavernous Cleveland Stadium was a nightmare for their offense. The outfield, one of only two in the league with symmetrical dimensions, was much larger than League Park's. It stretched 320 feet from home plate along the foul lines and extended 450 feet to the base of the center field bleacher wall. Except for line drives down the left- and right-field lines, virtually no hitters could reach the seats. The vast playing field caused Babe Ruth to joke in 1933 that "a guy ought to have a horse to play the outfield." The Indians suffered because of the new conditions. Center fielder Earl Averill, who had clobbered 32 home runs in 1932, hit only 11 in 1933. The team's batting average fell from .285 to .261, and the Indians scored 200 fewer runs. Their won-lost record also suffered; their 75-76 mark was the worst since 1928.

To the disappointment of city officials, the Indians in 1934 returned to League Park for the bulk of their home schedule. They did not return to the Stadium until 1936, when they held a single game there. Afterwards, they began to play games in the Stadium only on Sundays, holidays, and special occasions which might draw big crowds. One such occasion came on July 8, 1935, when the Stadium hosted the third annual All-Star game. A crowd of 69,831 came to the lakefront for the contest, an All-Star record which would stand for 46 years. Fans witnessed the American League post its third straight victory 4-1, as home-town favorite Mel Harder was credited with a game-saving relief appearance.

Another special event use of the Stadium occurred in 1937 during the Great Lakes Exposition. The Indians played ten extra games at the Stadium that summer and offered fans a double-header attraction. For an extra 25 cents, fans could buy a ticket which would not only admit them to the baseball game, but to the fairgrounds adjacent to the park. The promotion proved a major success; for the ten games, the Tribe drew 276,788 spectators. As a result, home attendance for the year was the best since 1926.

In 1939, night baseball at the Stadium gained an additional foothold on Indians' fans. Crosley Field in Cincinnati witnessed the first major league night game in 1935, but it was not until May 1939 that night baseball made it to the American League (at Shibe Park in Philadelphia). Since League Park had no field lighting, Cleveland Stadium, its lighting newly improved, became the site for all night baseball games. The Indians' first night game took place on the lakefront against the Detroit Tigers on June 27, 1939. Twenty-year-old Bob Feller, who had already become a star and major attraction for the Indians, started for the Tribe. On the last day of the 1938 season he had struck out 18 Detroit batters and was also able to prevent Hank

In 1935 Cleveland Stadium hosted the first of its four All-Star games. The facility holds the record for the three largest All-Star crowds. (Osborn Engineering Company)

Greenberg from tying Babe Ruth's single-season home run record of 60. Feller's night-time debut was nothing less spectacular, as he held the Tigers to one hit in a 5-0 victory in front of 53,035 fans.

The Tigers would get revenge on the Indians' ace the next year, however. At the end of the 1940 season, Feller participated in what may have been the most raucous game ever played at Municipal Stadium. Detroit came to Cleveland in late September for a season-ending showdown series in which the Indians could have

Always crowd-pleasers were Stadium old-timer games, which drew some of the greatest players of all time. Here, (left to right) Ty Cobb, Babe Ruth, and Tris Speaker enjoy a stadium moment in 1941. (Cleveland Press Collection of the Cleveland State University Archives)

clinched the pennant by winning all three games. A local radio station had urged listeners to attend the game to "get even" with Detroit fans for abusing the Indians. The ladies' day crowd of 48,533 fans came armed with bags of fruit, vegetables, and eggs. In the first inning, Tribe fans hurled what they had at left fielder Hank Greenberg when he tried to catch a fly ball. Seizing the microphone, umpire Bill Summers threatened to forfeit the game if the fans persisted. In the second inning, a fan dumped a basket of fruit and beer bottles over the upper deck railing in left field onto Tiger catcher Birdie Tebbetts, who was in the bullpen. He was knocked unconscious. Police tried to arrest the fan, and with that a brawl ensued. Indians' manager Oscar Vitt tried to calm fans over the Stadium public address system. When the responsible fan was finally brought to the visitors' clubhouse for identification, Tebbetts, revived but bruised, punched the fan repeatedly. The fan was taken to jail. Throughout the rest of the game, the crowd continued to throw eggs and other garbage at both the Indians and the Tigers players.

The game's outcome was as unfortunate as the circumstances surrounding it. Floyd Giebell, a veteran minor leaguer who would never win another major league game, outpitched Feller (even though the Indians' pitcher held Detroit to only three hits) and the Indians, 2-0, dashing the Tribe's pennant hopes and clinching the American League pennant for the Tigers. Cleveland won the final two games of the series, and finished second, one game out.

Bob Feller, an Iowan who had broken into the majors at age 17, was probably the Cleveland Indians' all-time greatest gate attraction. During his prime, his pitching appearances were one of the top draws in the major leagues. Signed to the Tribe for one dollar and an autographed baseball, he came to Cleveland in 1936, never having pitched in the minor leagues, and he took the baseball world by storm. In his first start he struck out 15 St. Louis Browns; a few weeks later, he set an American League record by striking out 17 A's. From then on, he never looked back. In 20 years with the Indians, he won 266 games and lost 162. During his career he led the American League in strikeouts seven times, struck out 2,581 batters, had six 20-victory seasons, and posted 46 shutouts. Impressive as they are, the figures might have been even more incredible had it not been for Feller's service to his country in World War II during the peak of his career. As a result, he missed the entire 1942, 1943, 1944, and almost all of the 1945 campaign. In 1941 he had won 25 games and in 1946, his first full season back, he chalked up another 26 victories while striking out 348 batters. Until the end of his career in 1956, Feller reigned as the preeminent hero in the hearts of Indians' fans. He was inducted to the Baseball Hall of Fame in 1962, his first year of eligibility, and in 1994 a statue of him was erected in the plaza outside the new Indians' ballpark.

Perhaps Feller's greatest rival at the box office was Yankee outfielder Joe DiMaggio. In 1941, DiMaggio's greatest accomplishment was to become indelibly

Bob Feller (right) became one of baseball's greatest attractions and one of the best players ever to don an Indians' uniform. Here he speaks with owner Bill Veeck and Indians' shortstop/ manager Lou Boudreau. (Cleveland Press Collection of the Cleveland State University Archives)

The Cleveland Indians–Memories of Hope, Memories of Despair

linked with Cleveland Stadium. That season, the Yankee Clipper, as he was called, was thrilling the baseball world with his consecutive-game hitting streak. The streak had begun on May 15, and it stood at 55 when the Yankees came to Cleveland for a three-game series in mid-July. The first game was played at League Park, which was no problem for DiMaggio as he collected three hits in four plate appearances. The streak stood at 56 games.

The second game was played on the night of July 17 at Cleveland Stadium in front of 67,468, the most ever for a night contest. Lefthander Al Smith started for the Tribe. He faced DiMaggio three times; in the Clipper's first at-bat, Cleveland third baseman Ken Keltner made a spectacular backhanded play to stop a hard shot and throw DiMaggio out at first; in his next at-bat Smith walked the Clipper (which drew boos from many in the crowd); in the seventh inning Keltner made another brilliant play from third base to get DiMaggio; and finally, in the ninth inning, facing reliever Jim Bagby and with the bases loaded, the Yankee star hit a ground ball to Indians' shortstop Lou Boudreau, who turned it into a rally-killing double play. So it was that the greatest hitting streak in the history of major league baseball came to an end in Cleveland Stadium.

The next day, DiMaggio started a brand new streak. He would hit safely in the next 16 consecutive contests. When that streak ended, the Yankee Clipper had hit in 72 of 73 games.

The World War II years were bleak ones for baseball. Many of its stars were away in service, and as a result major league attendance lagged everywhere. For Cleveland baseball, however, the war years paved the way for an exciting new era in Indians' baseball. After 19 years at the helm, owner Alva Bradley was ready to sell the team, and on June 21, 1946, Bill Veeck bought controlling interest. (At this time, Clevelander Bob Hope also purchased shares in the franchise.)

Wounded during the war, Veeck was hobbled by his injuries and often in considerable pain. Yet, those injuries belied his enthusiasm. A connoisseur in marketing and salesmanship, he constantly encouraged interest in the Tribe. His efforts paid off; attention to the team soared as did attendance. In 1946 the Indians passed the million mark for the first time. Confident in the team's potential, Veeck negotiated a new lease with the City of Cleveland that would make the Stadium the Tribe's full-time home. On September 21, 1946, the Indians played their last game ever at League Park.

One of the first changes Veeck made was to install an outfield fence at the Stadium. When originally proposed by Cleveland *Press* sports editor White Lewis to then-owner Bradley, the idea was not well received. Lewis was merely reiterating complaints that the players had made during their first full year of play at the Stadium in 1933. The field, they said, was simply too big. Too many line drives were caught, which led to lower batting averages for the hitters and to dull games for the fans. To Veeck, though, the idea of an outfield fence might make for more exciting games, which would draw more fans. So, just before the start of the 1947 season, the team installed a five-and-one-half-foot wire fence, which trimmed down the size of the outfield. The fence took 70 feet from what had been required to hit a home run to dead center. Veeck was excited about the fence and declared that the fence would stay permanently. "Now," he said, "our players will have a chance to hit some home runs at home like the Red Sox and Yankees."

The Indians also presented their new mascot for the 1947 campaign. Chief Wahoo, designed by Plain Dealer artist Fred Reinert, appeared on Tribe uniforms for the first time. The mascot, although periodically revised, has been a defining, though controversial, part of the team ever since.

With his innovative promotions Veeck was instrumental in attracting many baseball fans to Indians' games. The Wigwam, set up in the outfield at League Park, was one such attraction. (Cleveland Press Collection of the Cleveland State University Archives)

Standing-room-only crowds were frequent during the Tribe's attendance-record-setting 1948 season. The area behind the outfield fence, installed in 1947, allowed a few thousand extra fans to be admitted to the park for "big games." (Cleveland Press Collection of the Cleveland State University Archives)

Veeck showed his innovative spirit in a more substantial way as well. On July 3, 1947, he signed Larry Doby to a major league contract, and two days later Doby became the first black athlete to play for an American League team. In his ten-year career with Cleveland, he was a six-time all star, was named the game's best center fielder in 1950 by *The Sporting News*, and led the Indians with a .318 average during the 1948 World Series. His contributions on and off the field helped ease the way for equal opportunity for other black players in the league.

Another highlight of the 1947 season occurred exactly one week after Doby signed with the Tribe. Indians' pitcher Don Black tossed the first no-hit game in Cleveland Stadium history, as he beat the Philadelphia Athletics 3-0. Later that year, however, his moment of triumph was overshadowed by one of tragedy. On September 13 as he approached home plate for an at-bat, he began to reel dizzily and passed out. He was rushed to the hospital, where the medical staff diagnosed a cerebral hemorrhage. Miraculously, Black battled back and even managed to return to the mound briefly the next year. Despite his courage, though, he could not regain his old form, and after a few appearances early in 1948, his major league career came to an end.

For the rest of the Cleveland Indians, though, 1948 was a year of destiny. Encouraged by Veeck's promotions and the Tribe's play, home attendance had soared to over 1.5 million fans in 1947. As the 1948 season dawned, excitement filled the air and patrons flocked to Cleveland Stadium in record numbers. Crowds of 60,000-70,000 became commonplace as pennant fever gripped the city. The club set a season record for attendance at 2,620,627, which was not eclipsed until 1962 when the Dodgers drew 2,755,184 fans. Cleveland held the American League record until the 1980 Yankees attracted 2,627,417. The current American League record for home attendance, 4,057,947, was set by the Toronto Blue Jays in 1993. The 1993 Colorado Rockies hold the National League record with 4,483,350. The 1996 Indians, who sold out the season long before it opened, drew 3,318,174, which represents the all-time Cleveland baseball record.

On the field, the 1948 Indians were a stellar attraction. The team is perhaps the most revered and best remembered team in Cleveland Indians' history. Lou Boudreau, the team's popular shortstop-manager who had been at the helm since 1942, led the Tribe. In 1948 Boubreau had his best season, batting .355 and garnering the league's Most Valuable Player award. Boudreau would go on to be the winningest manager in Indians' history (from 1942–1950 he guided the team to 728 victories). Third baseman Ken Keltner contributed a .297 average, 31 home runs, and exciting defensive play while second baseman Joe Gordon batted .280, stroked 32 round trippers, and knocked in 124 runs. In the outfield, the Indians were led by Larry Doby, who roamed center field and posted a .301 batting average, and left fielder Dale Mitchell, who hit at a .336 clip.

The World Champion 1948 Cleveland Indians drew 2,620,627 fans to Municipal Stadium, an American League attendance record which stood until 1980. (Cleveland Indians)

Pitching proved also to be a strength of the 1948 Cleveland club. Feller, with 19 wins and an American League-leading 164 strikeouts, anchored the squad. Gene Bearden and Bob Lemon led the team with 20 wins apiece. They both led the AL in other important statistics as well: Bearden with a 2.43 earned run average and Lemon with 20 complete games. Arriving from the Negro Leagues and bolstering the mound crew at mid-season was the fabled Satchel Paige. At age 42, he was the oldest rookie ever to play in the major leagues. When Veeck signed Paige, he had been the greatest star in the Negro Leagues for 22 years, and he continued his success with the Indians in 1948. He finished the year with a 6-1 record, but also contributed in other ways during the stretch run. Whenever he pitched, he drew huge crowds. In his first start at Cleveland Stadium on August 3, 72,000 fans showed up to see him lead the club to a 4-3 victory over the Senators. His other wins included back-to-back shutouts over the Chicago White Sox, the second one before a Stadium crowd of 78,362, which remains the major league record for a night game. Overall, the team's pitchers led the American League in earned run average (3.22) and shutouts (26) and were a formidable crew for any opponent.

Despite their talent, the Indians found themselves in a tight pennant race at the end of the season in which every game counted. Perhaps the single most unforgettable moment in the thrilling season took place at the Stadium on August 8, in the first game of a doubleheader against the Yankees. Boudreau had been injured a few days earlier in a collision at second base and he scratched his name from the lineup because he was hampered by a strained right shoulder and a sprained left ankle. The Tribe was down in the game by two runs in the seventh inning, but they had loaded the bases with two out. From the dugout limped Boudreau to pinch hit. The announcement came over the loud speaker: "Batting for [Thurman] Tucker, number 5 ..." The noise of the 73,844 fans in attendance drowned out Boudreau's name. With the crowd watching tensely and cheering loudly, Boudreau delivered, stroking a single past the shortstop and scoring two runs to tie the game. The fans were in a frenzy. The momentum helped the home team take the first game, and then the nightcap as well. That was the kind of magic that made 1948 so memorable a year. The magic notwithstanding, the Tribe found itself tied with the Boston Red Sox for first place after the final game of the regular season had been completed. A one-game playoff was set to be played in Fenway Park. Cleveland was ready for the duel. The Indians clobbered the Sox 8-3, before a stunned Boston crowd who watched Indian hurler Gene Bearden craft a five-hitter and Boudreau stroke a two-run home run.

For the first time since 1920, the Cleveland Indians had made it to the World Series. Their opponents were Boston's National League team, the Braves. The first two games, played in Boston, left the teams tied in the series at one game apiece. The Tribe's loss was by a 1-0 score, even though Feller pitched a masterful two-hitter. The Brave's Phil Masi was the only runner to cross the plate that day, scoring after a much disputed call in which Feller had attempted to pick him off second base. The umpire ruled him safe, and Masi's run proved to be the game winner.

Municipal Stadium hosted the next three games, in which the Indians took the first two contests to take a 3-1 lead in the series. The fifth game on Sunday, October 10, drew a record 86,288 fans to the lakefront who were hoping to see the Indians wrap up the series in Cleveland. They left disappointed, as the Braves sent the series back to Boston by rocking Feller and compiling 12 hits in an 11-5 victory. In the sixth game, the Tribe won, 4-3, behind the pitching of Bob Lemon and the hitting of Joe Gordon and first baseman Eddie Robinson. The Cleveland Indians captured their second world championship, winning the series four games to two. A crowd of approximately 300,000 lined the street of downtown Cleveland to welcome their world champions home.

In 1949 the Indians again drew well, with 2,233,771 passing through the turnstiles at the Stadium, the second consecutive year in which the attendance topped two million and one of only three times that attendance at the Stadium hit that figure. Midway through the 1949 season, the short but fabled Bill Veeck era came to an end. He sold the Tribe to a syndicate headed by Ellis Ryan. That year, the Tribe finished in third place.

The 1950 season saw the Indians slip another notch in the standings, to fourth place. Although the Indians posted an impressive 92-62 record, the season was to be the last as manager for Boudreau, who headed to Boston. One of the highlights that year was the longest home run ever hit in Municipal Stadium. On June 23 Tribe first baseman Luke Easter powered a ball into the upper deck of Section 4, a distance of 477 feet from home plate. No ball was ever hit into the bleachers, although Mickey Mantle, Frank Howard, Rocky Colavito, and Jose Canseco all hit homers which hit or bounced near the bleacher wall, a distance of some 465 feet from the plate.

The World Championship crown is removed from Chief Wahoo at the end of the 1949 season. The Indians were still champs at the gate, however, drawing 2,223,771. (Cleveland Indians)

When Al Lopez took the helm as the Indians' new manager in 1951, he was to begin an era in which he established the best winning percentage of any Cleveland skipper in the team's history. Lopez, nicknamed the Señor, managed the team through the 1956 season and compiled a won-loss record of 570-354 (a .617 winning percentage). In his six years in Cleveland, Lopez steered the Tribe to five second-place finishes, all behind the New York Yankees, and in 1954 to their third American League championship. His feats in Cleveland and later in Chicago earned him a place in baseball's Hall of Fame.

The strong showing of the Tribe under Lopez's leadership paid off at the box office in the early 1950s, which encouraged the Indians to provide the fans with an additional attraction. In 1952, the club opened an Indians' Hall of Fame on the main concourse of the Stadium. Designed to honor the team's all-time greats, the museum over the course of the next twenty years enshrined the following: Steve O'Neill, Cy Young, Mel Harder, Bob Feller, Bob Lemon, Hal Trosky, Nap Lajoie, Kenny Keltner, Bill Bradley, Lou Boudreau, Joe Sewell, Joe Jackson, Earl Averill, Tris

Speaker, Satchel Paige, Jim Hegan, Elmer Flick, Larry Doby, and Stan Coveleski. While the Hall of Fame proved popular with the fans, the space was needed to hold television equipment. So in 1972 the organization transferred the memorabilia to the Ohio Baseball Museum in Springfield, Ohio (and later moved to Maumee).

In 1953 the Cleveland Indians were again sold, this time to a syndicate headed by Myron H. Wilson. His investment in the team was to bear fruit almost immediately, as the 1954 Tribe claimed the American League pennant with a record-setting 111 wins. To this day, no American League team has ever won as many games as did the 1954 Cleveland Indians. The 1906 Chicago Cubs hold the National League record of 116 wins.

The 1954 Tribe was anchored by an outstanding pitching staff. The "Big Four" starting rotation consisted of Early Wynn, Mike Garcia, Lemon, and Feller, while Art Houtteman contributed as the fifth starter. Dave Hoskins, Bob Hooper, former Detroit great Hal Newhouser, now in his twilight years, and two rookie stars named Don Mossi and Ray Narleski manned the bullpen. For the season, besides crafting 111 victories, the staff led the league with 77 complete games and a team earned-run-average of 2.78.

The 1954 Indians provided much excitement on their way to the American League pennant. Here, the Indians' Jim Hegan just misses tagging a sliding White Sox player. (William Nehez photo, Bruce Young collection)

The Indians could also do damage with their bats. For the fifth season in a row (and sixth in the last seven years), the team led the American League in home runs. Third baseman Al Rosen, who had garnered the American League MVP in 1953 by pounding 43 home runs and knocking in 145 runs, belted another 24 round-trippers, drove in 102 runs, and hit at a .300 clip. Doby contributed 32 homers and led the league with 126 RBIs. Newcomer Vic Wertz, who had battled his way back to professional baseball after a bout with polio, bolstered the team's power after being traded to Cleveland from Baltimore. Second baseman Bobby Avila captured the league's batting crown with a .341 average.

The Cleveland Indians—Memories of Hope, Memories of Despair

Despite a record-setting year of baseball and an incredible home record of 59-18, Stadium attendance in 1954 was not overwhelming. Attendance totaled only 1,355,472, or just over half of what it had been during the 1948 season. The reason for these lower numbers, however, is not clear. Perhaps Tribe fans had grown accustomed to watching the team play good ball until late in the season, when the Indians would falter and finish in second place. Cleveland fans, however, did set one new attendance record that season. On September 12, the largest crowd ever to watch a doubleheader, 84,587, saw the Tribe sweep the Yankees, their nearest challengers to first place.

During the 1954 season, Cleveland hosted its second All-Star Game. On July 13, a Stadium crowd of 68,751 had plenty to cheer about as the American League bested the National League in a slugfest, 11-9. Tribe fans saw Indians' hitters dominate the game, as Al Rosen clubbed a pair of home runs and Bobby Avila and Larry Doby combined for eight RBIs. The crowd remains the third largest ever to attend an All-Star game.

The 1954 World Series is one that most Indians' fans remember with frustration. Had Cleveland won that series, perhaps the 1954 Tribe might be considered one of the best teams ever to play in the major leagues. The outcome, however, was not to favor the Indians. Cleveland's pitching staff, which had performed so spectacularly during the regular season, was outhurled in the two opening games, which were played in New York's Polo Grounds. In the first game, Giant pinch-hitter Dusty Rhodes hit a three-run home run in the tenth inning to give New York the win. Willie Mays had helped send the game into extra innings with his famous over-the-shoulder catch of Vic Wertz's 460-foot drive in the eighth inning. The catch was the only time Wertz had been retired by Giant pitchers all day, as he went four for five. Then in the second game, although the Early Wynn and Don Mossi

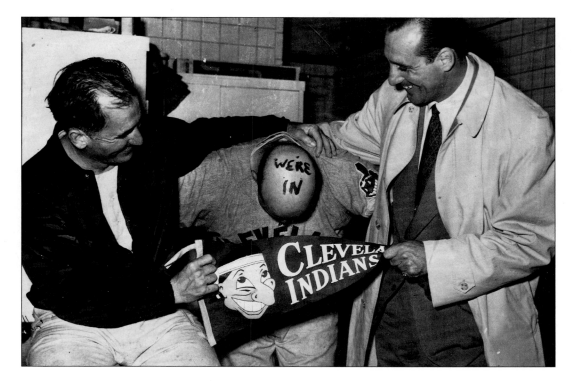

Popular first baseman Vic Wertz helps manager Al Lopez (left) and general manager Hank Greenberg (right) celebrate the Tribe's clinching the 1954 pennant. (Cleveland Press Collection of the Cleveland State University Archives)

combined to four-hit the Giants, the Indians lost 3-1. The third and fourth games were played in Municipal Stadium, and crowds of 71,555 and 78,102 watched the Giants jump out to early leads which they never relinquished. In the third game, Dusty Rhodes again hurt the Indians, delivering a two-run single in the third inning that led New York to a 6-2 victory. Game four featured the Giants building a seven-run lead, pacing them to a 7-4 win and making them the second National League team ever to sweep the World Series. The powerful Indians had fallen.

The Cleveland teams of 1955 and 1956 held onto second place. The club seemed to have found a key to continued success with an impressive young pitcher named Herb Score. A southpaw, Score compiled a 16-10 record during his rookie season of 1955 and improved the following year by amassing a 20-9 record, striking out a league-leading 263 batters, and posting a 2.53 ERA.

The next year was a fateful one for the Indians. William R. Daley, for an investment of $3,961,800, became the Tribe's new chief stockholder, although Mike Wilson remained in office as club president. The new ownership, however, would soon feel a franchise-wrenching jolt.

Score began the 1957 season in superb form, striking out 39 batters in his first 36 innings. On May 7, tragedy struck. In a game against the New York Yankees

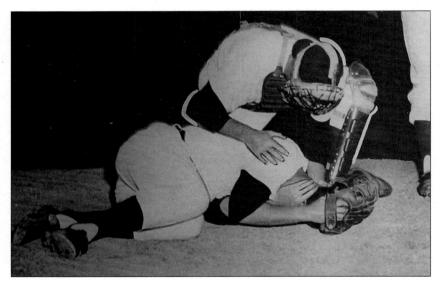

Tribe fortunes began to turn sour when Herb Score, the Indians' talented southpaw hurler, was struck in the eye by a line drive. While the injury curtailed a promising diamond career, Score remained an integral part of Cleveland's baseball scene as the Indians' perennial radio voice. (Cleveland Press photo, Jim Toman collection)

at Municipal Stadium, Score was on the mound, facing Gil McDougald. McDougald lined a Score pitch back to the mound, but before the hurler could react, the ball struck him in the right eye. Score was carried off the field on a stretcher, and although he returned to the team in 1958, he never regained his pre-injury form. That May evening at the Stadium proved fateful to the promising career for the young hurler.

In some ways, Score's injury seemed to mirror the troubles that soon became endemic in the Wigwam. In 1957 the Tribe's fortunes took a turn for the worse. Attendance fell to 722,256, the team's lowest since 1945. Worse, the team finished in sixth place. At 76-77, the Indians were under .500 for the first time in 11 years. One of the few positive aspects of the season was a re-landscaping of the area behind the fence. At the base of the bleacher wall, the team had shrubbery planted, and the centerpiece of the new look was a little waterfall. In 1958 Frank Lane replaced Hank Greenberg as the Indians' general manager. Greenberg had shown interest in moving the Indians to another city, but Daley chose to keep the team in Cleveland but move general managers. Lane's arrival heralded a new era of sweeping player trades, as his nickname "Trader Lane" indicated. From December 1957 to December 1959, he made 60 separate deals involving players. In 1959 the Indians gave Chicago a run for the pennant, but finished in second place, five games out; the exciting race, however, had brought 1,497,976 fans to the lakefront Stadium, the most in eight years.

In retrospect, the 1959 season was the "last hurrah" for the Cleveland Indians for quite some time. As the most successful decade of Tribe baseball came to a close, winning seasons became far less common. In 1960, just before the season opened, Lane traded Rocky Colavito, the team's most popular player, to Detroit for outfielder Harvey Kuenn. Not since the Indians had started play in the Stadium had a trade so enraged fans. Some came to refer to the subsequent 40-plus years of pennant-less Indians' seasons as the "Curse of Rocky Colavito." To many, the slugger's departure symbolized the demise of the team, and in their view "trader" Lane was more aptly named "traitor" Lane. Midway through the 1959 campaign, Lane even traded managers, sending Joe Gordon to Detroit for Jimmie Dykes. Nothing helped, however; Cleveland slipped into fourth place, and attendance dropped by almost a half-million.

In 1961 Gabe Paul replaced Frank Lane as general manager, and in 1962 he bought controlling interest in the Indians. He served as team president through 1971, and then moved to New York. He returned to Cleveland in 1978 and served as Tribe president through the 1984 season. Altogether Paul occupied a key position with the team for 17 years, an executive longevity exceeded only by Alva Bradley (1928-1946). During these years ownership of the franchise changed hands several times. In 1967 Vernon Stouffer took over the ownership reins from Paul while Paul remained club president. From 1972 until 1976, Nick Mileti headed an ownership syndicate and occupied the president's chair, and Ted Bonda followed up as chief during 1977 and 1978. Business and civic leader F.J. (Steve) O'Neill bought controlling interest in 1978, and the Tribe remained in his control (or that of his estate) through the 1986 season.

The Gabe Paul era was not marked with much success, either at the box office or on the field. Even the 1962 addition of a large Chief Wahoo on the Stadium roof just above Gate D did not help. Despite the Chief's beckoning smile, attendance lagged. Between 1960 and 1980, the Indians reached the million mark in attendance only three times (1974, 1979, 1980). The team only finished as high as third place once (in 1968, the Indians benefited from outstanding seasons by Sam McDowell and Luis Tiant) and in fourth place only three times (1974, 1975, 1976). During the Gabe Paul era, the Indians saw thirteen managers lead the team, but they managed to finish within eleven games behind the division winner only once (in the strike-shortened season of 1981 when the Tribe finished 52-51, seven games back).

Cleveland fans voted their "most memorable" baseball thrill the day that Cleveland player/manager Frank Robinson hit a home run in his first at-bat as an Indian. Here John Lowenstein congratulates the jubilant skipper on his spectacular debut, April 8, 1975. (Paul Tepley photo)

Those years, however, were not without many memorable moments and baseball thrills at the Stadium. On July 31, 1963, for instance, the Tribe tied a major league record by hitting four consecutive home runs against the Los Angeles Angels. It happened during the second game of an Indians' doubleheader sweep, when Woodie Held, Pedro Ramos (Cleveland's starting pitcher for the second game), Tito Francona, and Larry Brown each went deep. Also that season Clevelanders welcomed back to the Tribe old-favorite Early Wynn, who notched his 300th career victory against the Kansas City Athletics on July 13 at the Stadium. Two years later, Tribe fans welcomed back Rocky Colavito after a five-year absence from the team. The former hero rewarded his loyal fans by hitting a home run in his first game back as an Indian. Despite hitting a major-league-record 133 round trippers at Municipal Stadium in 1970, Cleveland still ended up in fifth place.

During the 1960s and into the 1970s, the Tribe had its share of stars, but it rarely experienced much team success. Luis Tiant won 21 games and earned a league-leading 1.60 ERA in 1968. "Sudden" Sam McDowell led the league in strikeouts four times in the 1960s, and in 1965 struck out 325 batters (the most ever by a Tribe southpaw), led the league with a 2.18 ERA, and threw two consecutive one-hitters. Gaylord Perry brought the Cy Young award to Cleveland in 1972 with a 24-win season. Ultimately, however, lack of organizational and financial stability forced the franchise to emphasize immediate benefits rather than long-term planning. When Colavito returned to Cleveland in 1965, the Indians gave up Tommy John and Tommie Agee. Stars like Rookie of the Year (1972) Chris Chambliss and Craig Nettles were traded without much concern for future team development.

As a part of baseball's bicentennial salute to the nation in 1976, fans in each city were asked to vote for the most memorable moment in their franchise's history. Cleveland fans selected an event which had taken place on opening day 1975. That year Frank Robinson made his debut as the Indians' player-manager, the first African American ever to pilot a major league team. The Tribe opened the 1975 campaign on a chilly April 8 at Municipal Stadium against the rival New York Yankees. In his very first at-bat as a Cleveland Indian, Robinson blasted a Doc Medich fastball over the left field fence for a home run. As he rounded the bases, the crowd of 56,204, fully appreciating the significance of his swing, jumped to their feet and cheered the "most memorable" moment in Indians' history.

Another exceptional feat at the Stadium took place on May 15, 1981. The Tribe was hosting the Toronto Blue Jays that day, and on the mound for the Indians was 25-year-old Len Barker. And Barker was perfect. He completed his masterpiece in just 103 pitches, and never once went to a three-ball count on any batter. The Blue Jays hit only two fair balls solidly all night, but the Indians' defense protected Barker's efforts. Center fielder Rick Manning tracked down a line drive to the outfield, and second baseman Duane Kuiper successfully backhanded a hard one-hopper. The Indians won the game, 3-0. Barker's perfect game was only the tenth perfect game in major league history, and the first since 1968. Although there were a total of nine no-hitters pitched at the Stadium, Barker's was the only one that was perfect.

Another highlight of the 1981 season was the annual All-Star Game. Major League Baseball had awarded the game to Cleveland Stadium to commemorate the facility's fiftieth anniversary. The 1981 All-Star game marked the fourth time the

The Cleveland Indians—Memories of Hope, Memories of Despair

Stadium hosted the summer classic. Originally, the contest was to have been played on July 14, but a 49-day player strike forced it to be rescheduled for Sunday evening, August 9. Perhaps starved for baseball by the strike, 72,086 fans turned out to see the game. It was the largest crowd in All-Star Game history, and it saw the National League edge the American League, 5-4. With that game, Cleveland held the record for the top three All-Star crowds in baseball history.

Three years later, some late-season heroics took place at the lakefront. Although the 1984 Indians were en route to another disappointing campaign, they provided excitement two games in a row in a season-ending series against Minnesota to drop the Twins from the pennant race. On September 27, Jamie Quirk, who had been obtained as an emergency catcher the night before, smacked a pinch hit home run in the bottom of the ninth with two outs, giving the Tribe a 4-3 win. The next night, the Indians found themselves down 10-0 after three innings. Led by Brett Butler, Joe Carter, and Andre Thornton, the Tribe clawed its way back to defeat the Twins 11-10 in the bottom of the ninth.

The Indians' perennial failure to mount a serious challenge for the pennant and the attendant dismal gate receipts forced the Tribe's management to look to promotions to provide some thrills missing from the diamond itself. Of course, promotions—baseball purists might call them "stunts"—have not been a phenomenon only of the years of frustration.

On May 15, 1981, Len Barker hurled the first and only perfect game in Cleveland Stadium history as the Indians beat the Toronto Blue Jays, 3-0. (Paul Tepley photo)

Bill Veeck's masterful promotions drew many fans to the lakefront Stadium. He sponsored all kinds of giveaways, one even held to honor the "ordinary fan," in which one lucky patron went home laden with prizes.

Perhaps Veeck's most famous stunt involved hiring baseball magician Jackie Price. First and foremost, Price was an acrobat. He could throw three balls with one motion. He could bat upside down. He could even hit a high pop fly, jump into a Jeep, race after it, and make the catch. His antics provided the fans with many a laugh.

Promotions have always included the more conservative, such as old-timer games or bat or helmet giveaway days. One more imaginative giveaway took place in 1975 when the field was strewn with money and selected contestants were given 90 seconds to scramble for it. Other promotions involved hiring an act to perform

Bat Day was another sure-fire method for packing the stands. Here thousands of youngsters testify to their approval of the promotion. (Cleveland Indians)

before, during, or after the regularly scheduled baseball games. Some of the acts hired by the Indians have been real daredevils.

In 1974 Hugo Zucchini was blasted out of a cannon. In both 1974 and 1975 high-wire artist Karl Wallenda provided his brand of aerial thrill. A wire was stretched 700 feet across the field 115 feet above the turf. Then Wallenda took his daring walk. Midway through his trek, he paused, performed a headstand, and resumed his walk to the other side. The feat took fifteen minutes. He later explained that performing his routine at the Stadium entailed an additional challenge. The winds which circled in from the open end of the park, he said, had brought an extra element of risk. (In 1981 the Indians had another aerial artist walk the wire; Jay Cochrane did it on June 3.)

Another acrobatic act took Wallenda's performance one step closer to danger in 1977. The Vashek Duo rode a motorcycle across the high wire. As Vashek maneuvered the craft across the cable, his wife swung breezily from a trapeze suspended from the cycle. Then there was A.J. Bakunas. He leaped from the Stadium roof onto an inflated nylon bag which measured 18 feet by 25 feet. The velocity of his daring fall was measured at 96 miles per hour.

The Indians' management tried another kind of promotion during the mid-1980s. A variation of the double header, this event featured professional wrestling as the second half of the bill. The matches, sanctioned by the National Wrestling Alliance, were staged in a ring set up at second base. On July 13, 1986, 31,150 fans were on hand for the event. The next year, the second match attracted 17,864.

The Tribe also tried various combinations of music and baseball to attract fans to Municipal Stadium. During the 1980s the Indians invited several musical acts to perform on the field after a game, including Joe Walsh, the Beach Boys, and Crosby,

The Cleveland Indians–Memories of Hope, Memories of Despair

Stills & Nash. Country stars Charlie Daniels and Ronnie Milsap also appeared on the Indians' post-game stages.

While most of the promotions were fun and gave baseball fans additional entertainment for their admission dollars, one promotion did not turn out the way planners had hoped. As a result, the city's reputation became sorely tainted. On June 4, 1974, 25,134 turned out for "Beer Night," at which the beverage cost a dime per cup. As a result, some fans consumed too much, and inebriation led to a minor riot during the bottom half of the ninth inning as the Indians battled the Texas Rangers. Oddly, the Indians had just rallied to tie the score and the winning run was on third base with two outs. After repeated indiscretions against the players throughout the game, fans vaulted from the stands and mobbed Ranger right fielder Jeff Burroughs. Perhaps some were "inspired" by a brawl between the two teams the previous week in a game at Texas, but most were simply reeling from inebriation. The presence of the fans on the field brought all the players from both teams out of the dugouts. Many Rangers, including manager Billy Martin, wielded bats. Many fights broke out between Rangers and the fans, causing umpire Nestor Chylak to forfeit the game to Texas. The American League forced the Indians to cancel the other three Beer Nights scheduled that season. The fans' behavior that night is still remembered, and it has remained a smudge on the history of a grand field.

However much promotions appealed to fans, fundamentally they come to the park to watch the game and cheer on their team. The inability of the Indians to win consistently had its impact on fan support for the franchise. For instance, in the 25 years between 1960 and 1985, the Tribe topped the one million mark in annual attendance only four times (1974, 1979, 1980, and 1982). The reality of the circumstances were underscored in April 1986 when American League President Bobby Brown was quoted as saying that "the situation in Cleveland is precarious." His statement came on the heels of a 1985 season in which the team had tied its all-time record for losses, tasting defeat 102 times and finishing in last place, 39-1/2 games back. Only 655,181 fans had come to the Stadium to watch the ineptitude. In addition to these depressing realities, the franchise's destiny was on the auction block. Numerous rumors of an impending move to Tampa Bay or St. Petersburg circulated. The team was then being overseen by a trustee of the estate of its late owner, F.J. O'Neill, who had died in 1983. It seemed to many that Cleveland's continuing status as a founding member of the American League was in jeopardy.

But perhaps Bobby Brown's words were a catalyst for revival. The very next day after the league president's story had been run in *The Plain Dealer*, Cleveland Mayor George Voinovich launched a civic campaign to boost the Indians' support. His Citizens' Night on May 23, 1986, brought 61,340 to the Stadium to see the Tribe beat the Blue Jays, 3-1. Aided by an early-season winning streak of ten games, the attendance continued to soar. On July 4, for instance, a crowd of 73,303 came to the ballpark. The Tribe blasted the Royals that day, 10-3.

The 1986 season energized the many baseball fans who made it to the lakefront, and with good reason. While the team ended up in fifth place, it finished the closest to the division winner an Indians' team had in a full season since 1959 (11-1/2 games back) and achieved the best winning percentage since 1968 (84-78, .519). In addition, the team, loaded with such offensive stars as Joe Carter, Brett Butler, Pat Tabler, Julio Franco, and Cory Snyder, led the league in batting average, slugging percentage, runs, hits, triples, and stolen bases. The exciting play on the field helped to draw renewed interest in the Tribe.

When the final turnstile count was totalled for 1986, the figure stood at 1,471,977, the best since 1959. Then two months later, the team was sold to Richard and David Jacobs for a reputed $34 million. The Jacobs brothers, Clevelanders with "deep pockets" and strong loyalties to their city, gave the franchise renewed spirit and stability. Tribe president Peter Bavasi, whose short tenure had been marked by angry fan reaction to his plan to close the Stadium bleachers, resigned. He was replaced by Hank Peters.

Because of Cleveland's earlier record attendance support, baseball pundits had talked about the city as a "sleeping giant." The theory was that if the fans got a team to really cheer about, they would once again flock to Indians' games in record numbers. The "sleeping giant" stirred a bit in 1986, and in the seven subsequent years of Jacobs' ownership, attendance remained above the million mark. While crowd support improved during the 1990s, the Tribe's final standings remained familiar: two fourths, one sixth, and one seventh place finish.

Yet, there was reason for fans to hope. Mike Hargrove, who had piloted numerous minor league Tribe teams to championships, became the Indians' manager

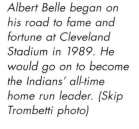

Albert Belle began on his road to fame and fortune at Cleveland Stadium in 1989. He would go on to become the Indians' all-time home run leader. (Skip Trombetti photo)

midway during the 1991 season, and John Hart was named general manager following that season. The Indians' management undertook a plan to attract a crop of talented young players to the team, and more importantly, to sign them to long-term contracts. The organization also focused on improving its minor league system in order to develop more quality players within the franchise. On the field, the team became more exciting to watch, and the promise of player stability gave fans renewed hope for the future.

Increased fan support was also spurred by the Indians' intended move to a new baseball-only park at Gateway, which voters approved in 1990. Many came to believe that the opening of a new ballpark would also mean the dawn of a new era of competitiveness.

Nostalgia for the Stadium also played a key role in the resurgence of fan interest, as support in the team soared during 1993, which was the Tribe's last year at the lakefront park. The season began on a tragic note with one of the worst accidents to afflict a major league baseball team. Indians' pitchers Steve Olin and Tim Crews were killed and Bob Ojeda seriously injured in a boating accident during spring training in Florida.

For the fans, the terrible loss served only to intensify their loyalty and backing

The early 1990s were not kind to the Indians. Weak play meant weak crowds. The sleeping giant had not yet awakened. (Skip Trombetti photo)

for the team. It was in 1994, after all, at Gateway, that the Indians would rise from the decades of defeat. The 1993 season was but a prelude to that new era. It was also one last time to relive the memories of 61 years of Stadium baseball. Indians' management marketed the season with a series of promotions featuring giveaway items keyed to the Tribe's history, and attendance climbed. The final and much heralded three-game series finale at the Stadium against the Chicago White Sox on October 1-3, was an early sellout.

Though the Indians lost those last three games, it did not seem to matter much to the fans. They came for the memories. And the final series was replete with nostalgia. Game opening and closing festivities were elaborate. Dozens of Indians' greats from the past were introduced on the field. Friday night's game ended with a ceremonial final turning off of the Stadium's baseball field lights, one bank at a time. Sunday's final farewell was particularly poignant. After the game, 83-year-old Mel Harder, who had thrown the first pitch in Municipal Stadium in 1932, delivered a final ceremonial throw to the plate. Cleveland favorite and one-time part team owner, Bob Hope, sang a special version of his theme song, "Thanks for the Memories." And then home plate was removed–the only part of the Stadium field to move to the new park.

During the final series, more than 215,000 fans came to the Stadium to pay their final respects to the Indians' lakefront home. Many tears were shed and memories relived. It was the passing of an era.

The Tribe's 1993 attendance totalled 2,177,908, third highest in team history and the most since 1949. It brought the team's attendance in its full seasons at the Stadium (1933, and 1947-1993) to 50,872,158, a season average of 1,067,923.

Altogether, including the part-time years at the Stadium, the Indians played 4,189 games in the lakefront park, winning 2,235 of them for a .534 winning percentage. The team had winning home records during 35 of its 47 seasons on the lakefront.

Although the Cleveland Indians lost both the first and last game ever played at Municipal Stadium, the history of the years in between transcend the numbers in the win column. The facility's durability and fixed presence on the lakefront became the stage for many baseball dramas: tears of elation and frustration, proud and unifying moments in the city's civic history, significant moments in the annals of major league baseball, and for any fans who ever saw a game at the Stadium, special memories fixed forever in their minds.

On April 4, 1994, the Cleveland Indians began a new era at Jacobs Field. Opening day was a sellout, and the gleaming new ballpark brought raves from the fans. Better yet, the first game was a come-from-behind victory, stirring hopes that the inaugural was a positive portent of things to come.

The final Indians' game at the Stadium was held on a bright Sunday afternoon, October 3, 1993. A poignant closing moment took place following the game when Bob Hope sang a rendition of "Thanks for the Memories." (David Kachinko photo)

The Cleveland Indians–Memories of Hope, Memories of Despair

CLEVELAND INDIANS' MANAGERS
THE STADIUM YEARS, 1932-1993

MANAGER	YEARS AS SKIPPER	WON-LOSS RECORD (Winning Percentage)
Roger Peckinpaugh*	1928-1933, 1941	490-481 (.505)
Walter Johnson*	1933-1935	180-168 (.517)
Steve O'Neill*	1935-1937	199-168 (.542)
Oscar Vitt*	1938-1940	262-190 (.570)
Lou Boudreau*	1942-1950	728-649 (.529)
Al Lopez	1951-1956	570-354 (.617)
Kerby Farrell	1957	76-77 (.497)
Bobby Bragan	1958	31-36 (.463)
Joe Gordon	1958-1961	184-151 (.549)
Jimmie Dykes	1960-1961	104-114 (.477)
Mel McGaha	1962	80-82 (.494)
Birdie Tebbets	1963-1966	311-298 (.511)
George Strickland	1966	15-25 (.385)
Joe Adcock	1967	75-87 (.463)
Alvin Dark	1968-1971	266-321 (.453)
John Lipon	1971	18-41 (.305)
Ken Aspromonte	1972-1974	220-260 (.458)
Frank Robinson	1975-1977	186-189 (.496)
Jeff Torborg	1977-1979	157-201 (.439)
Dave Garcia	1979-1982	247-244 (.503)
Mike Ferraro	1983	40-60 (.400)
Pat Corrales	1983-1987	280-355 (.441)
Doc Edwards	1987-1989	172-207 (.454)
John Hart	1989	8-11 (.421)
John McNamara	1990-1991	102-137 (.427)
Mike Hargrove	1991-1993	204-225 (.476)

*Managed home games at both Cleveland Stadium and League Park.

INDIANS' RECORD AND ATTENDANCE
CLEVELAND STADIUM YEARS

SEASON	STADIUM W-L	OVERALL W-L	FINISH	STADIUM ATTENDANCE
1933	45-32	75-76	4TH	387,936
1947	39-39	80-74	4TH	1,521,978
1948	48-30	97-58	1ST	2,620,627
1949	49-28	89-65	3RD	2,233,771
1950	49-28	92-62	4TH	1,727,464
1951	53-24	93-61	2ND	1,704,984
1952	49-28	93-61	2ND	1,444,607
1953	53-24	92-62	2ND	1,069,176
1954	59-18	111-43	1ST	1,335,472
1955	49-28	93-61	2ND	1,221,780
1956	46-31	88-66	2ND	865,467
1957	40-39	76-77	6TH	722,256
1958	42-34	77-76	4TH	663,805
1959	43-34	89-65	2ND	1,497,976
1960	39-38	76-78	4TH	950,985
1961	40-41	78-83	5TH	725,547
1962	43-38	80-82	6TH	716,076
1963	41-40	79-83	5TH	562,507
1964	41-40	79-83	6TH	653,293
1965	52-30	87-75	5TH	934,786
1966	41-40	81-81	5TH	903,359
1967	36-45	75-87	8TH	667,623
1968	43-37	86-75	3RD	857,994
1969	33-48	62-99	6TH	619,970
1970	43-38	76-86	5TH	729,752
1971	29-52	60-102	6TH	591,361
1972	43-34	72-84	5TH	759,871
1973	34-47	71-91	6TH	605,073
1974	40-41	77-85	4TH	1,114,262
1975	41-39	79-80	4TH	977,039
1976	44-35	81-78	4TH	948,776
1977	37-44	71-90	5TH	900,365

The Cleveland Indians–Memories of Hope, Memories of Despair

INDIANS' RECORD AND ATTENDANCE
CLEVELAND STADIUM YEARS

SEASON	STADIUM W-L	OVERALL W-L	FINISH	STADIUM ATTENDANCE
1978	42-36	69-90	6TH	800,584
1979	47-34	81-80	6TH	1,011,644
1980	40-35	79-81	6TH	1,033,872
1981	25-29	52-51	6TH	661,395
1982	41-40	78-84	6TH	1,044,021
1983	36-45	70-92	7TH	768,941
1984	41-39	75-87	6TH	734,269
1985	38-43	60-102	7TH	655,181
1986	45-35	84-78	5TH	1,471,977
1987	35-46	61-101	7TH	1,077,898
1988	44-37	78-84	6TH	1,411,610
1989	41-40	73-89	6TH	1,285,542
1990	41-40	77-85	4TH	1,225,241
1991	30-52	57-105	7TH	1,051,863
1992	41-40	76-86	4TH	1,224,274
1993	46-35	76-86	6TH	2,177,908

Note: The Stadium hosted World Series games in 1948 and 1954. Attendance for these five games was 388,148. The Stadium also hosted some Indians' games 1936-1946. During these years, the team played 402 games at the Stadium and were 218-184.

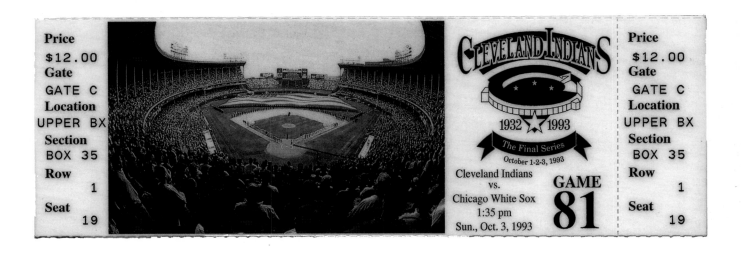

THE CLEVELAND BROWNS
A STORIED TRADITION

Few people in Cleveland can still remember the time when professional football in Cleveland meant anything other than the men in the brown and orange. The Browns' tradition means so much to Cleveland fans that even after Browns' president Art Modell took his team to Baltimore in 1996, the City and the fans fought to save the team colors, name, and records. Those belonged in Cleveland. Even though events forced the Browns' franchise to take a hiatus from their blustery lakefront home in 1996, the team and Municipal Stadium were National Football League fixtures for half a century, and their achievements were the stuff of legend. Yet, time was when other professional football organizations monopolized the attention of Cleveland sports fans.

The city's first involvement in professional football dates back to 1920, around the time the National Football League, then known as the American Professional Football Association, was being organized. The formation of the new league meant the beginning of standardized competition in what had been, up to that point, a club sport.

For two years (1920 and 1921) Cleveland fielded a squad in the fledgling league. With a borrowed name from the other professional franchise in the city, the football Indians folded by 1922. In 1923 the team tried to make another successful bid for permanence, reorganizing itself and playing to a 3-1-3 record. But, the team was not able to make the venture profitable.

The following year, Cleveland benefited at the expense of nearby Canton, Ohio, when Cleveland mogul Samuel Deutsch purchased that city's 1923 league-champion Bulldogs. He decided to move the team north to take advantage of the Forest City's potentially larger fan base. Playing their games at Dunn Field, the 1924 Bulldogs proved to be an exciting team, and finished the season with a 7-1-1 record, repeating as the NFL champions. While the squad brought home the championship, the team's dismal financial showing made their existence precarious. The Bulldogs were financially able to play only one more season, finishing 5-8-1 in 1925.

More failed attempts marked Cleveland's ventures into professional football. A year after the Bulldogs folded, area businessman Charles Zimmerman risked some capital to organize a team to compete in the newly formed American Football League. The Panthers, which played their games at Luna Park, an amusement park at Woodland and Woodhill roads, were not able to complete even one full season of play before financial troubles killed the franchise. Samuel Deutsch, however, made a second bid to establish an NFL team in Cleveland in 1927, but he again met with the same fate as he and the others had experienced. The city was then without a professional football team until 1931, when another Indians team was fielded. This third Indians' team played only that one year and finished 2-8. It did etch its name, though, in Cleveland Stadium history by being the first professional team to play there; they beat their semi-pro Pennzoil opponents, 10-0 in an exhibition game on September 9.

Five years passed until Damon Wetzel and Homer Marshman organized a squad to compete in a new American Football League. Their Cleveland Rams put together a 5-2-2 season in 1936, earning them a second place finish in the new league. The team's success prompted the owners to seek a franchise in the older NFL, and they completed the transfer in time for the 1937 season. The team found victories harder to come by, as the competition was considerably tougher in the by-then established NFL. Using League Park as their home field, the Rams were only able to manage one win in 11 games.

The Rams improved their record in 1938, but they only drew an average of approximately 5,000 fans per game at League Park. In order to stimulate attendance, team owners decided to move the squad's games to the lakefront field for the 1939

The 1945 edition of the Cleveland Rams was getting ready for a season that would take them to the NFL championship. Following the season, owner Dan Reeves announced he was moving the team to Los Angeles in 1946. (Cleveland Press Collection of the Cleveland State University Archives)

campaign. In their first season at Municipal Stadium, the Rams improved their record to .500, and attendance began to increase. The worst crowd that season was 6,085, and the best totaled 25,696. Two years later, Dan Reeves and Frederick Levy bought the team. In 1943, however, the new owners were summoned to serve in the armed forces, and because of their own absence and the diminishing supply of player talent, they requested and received permission to suspend the

franchise for that season (the Pittsburgh and Philadelphia franchises, similarly affected, combined their squads that year and were nicknamed the Steagles).

The team resumed play without much success in 1944 and was again calling League Park home. In 1945, though, fortunes began to turn. Rookie quarterback Bob Waterfield led the Rams, which early in the season proved they were a serious contender for the league title. As the team met with success on the field, attendance began to rise as well, putting League Park to the test. To accommodate the larger crowds, League Park officials added some temporary seating. On November 11, 1945, a large and enthusiastic crowd was on hand to watch the Rams. The weight and movement of the crowd became too much for the temporary seating, and the stands separated and collapsed, injuring 31 people.

The Rams went on to win their division. Because of the seating mishap at League Park, team officials, anticipating a sizeable crowd, scheduled the championship game with the Washington Redskins at Municipal Stadium. Frigid temperatures and biting winds affected the attendance for the season's final game, however, as only 32,178 braved the weather and watched the game. Those that went saw an exciting contest in which the Rams edged the Redskins 15-14, earning Cleveland its second NFL championship.

Much like what would happen 49 years later, the Rams' owner made a numbing announcement to Cleveland fans, who were still reveling in the Rams' title. On January 12, 1946, Dan Reeves informed the community that he was moving the franchise to Los Angeles. Many Clevelanders reacted as though they had been betrayed, but the financial facts seemed clear. Even though the Rams had captured the NFL championship, the team operated about $40,000 in debt. In their nine years in Cleveland, the Rams had not generated adequate fan support to keep the franchise afloat.

While many Clevelanders expressed deep anger at the loss of their NFL champion Rams, another development helped lessen the blow. On March 20, 1945, Arthur B. McBride, owner of the city's Yellow Cab Company, had announced that he would sponsor a Cleveland entry into the then-forming All-American Football Conference (AAFC). The league was set to begin play in 1946. Almost from the time of McBride's first announcement, the local media devoted as much coverage to the emergence of the new team as they did to the established Rams. Undoubtedly the threat of competition for football fans' time, money, and devotion helped Reeves, who had long sought to play on the West Coast, decide on making the move to Los Angeles.

Paul Brown was named to coach the city's new entry into the All-American Football Conference in 1946. He went on to become the most successful coach in Cleveland Browns' history. (Cleveland Press Collection of the Cleveland State University Archives)

McBride had actually begun assembling the foundations for the team before his official announcement. On February 5, 1945, the first head coach of the embryonic franchise was signed to a five-year, $125,000 contract, the most ever for a coach in professional football at the time. The new on-field leader was familiar to area football fans. As the head coach of the nearby Massillon High School Tigers, his teams had won six consecutive Ohio scholastic championships and all but one of the 60 games he coached. He moved on to coach the Ohio State Buckeyes for three successful years from 1941-43, earning one national championship. During the war years he served as coach of the Great Lakes Naval Academy team in Chicago. The 37-year-old coach was Paul Brown, who would leave an indelible mark on the history of the franchise and the city of Cleveland.

While the new AAFC squad was forming, McBride sought a name for the team. To help choose its name, he formed a select committee, which chose "Panthers" as the new moniker. But, because that name had been the property of the city's 1926 entry in the AFL and the previous owners still held the rights to it, "Panthers" was rejected. McBride and other organization officials decided to take matters into their own hands in August 1945 and chose "Browns" as the nickname. He then awarded a

The Cleveland Browns–A Storied Tradition

$1,000 War Bond to the man who wrote the best essay describing why the squad should be called the Browns. The winner explained that it was because of the team's famous new coach.

Almost from the start, Brown proved to be a fan favorite. Before the first season started, he declared openly that he sought to prove to the nation that Cleveland was an excellent sports town. He believed the fans were just waiting for a winner to support, and he hoped to provide that outlet:

> It's always been my contention that [Cleveland] can be developed into one of the hottest sports towns in the country. All the fans need is a winner....It is my intention to give them their money's worth for the next five years.

With Municipal Stadium as home, the Browns opened their inaugural 1946 season with a September 6 night game against the Miami Seahawks. From that first game, the level of fan support for the Browns became indicative of how much Greater Clevelanders would accept and support the team over time. A crowd of 60,135 went to the lakefront to see the Browns rout Miami, 44-0. At the time, it was the largest crowd ever to have witnessed a professional football game. With it, a new tradition of fan loyalty also emerged in the Greater Cleveland area.

The winning formula that began the era of Browns' football continued throughout the 1946 season. Paul Brown's hand-picked team proved to be one with many stars. He had signed former Northwestern University star Otto Graham as his quarterback, and he provided him with superb receivers in Mac Speedie and Dante Lavelli (soon to be known as "Glue Fingers"). Marion Motley was a bruising running back. Bill Willis was an all-star at guard, as was Lou Groza at tackle and Frank Gatski at center. Today Gatski, Graham, Groza, Lavelli, Motley, and Willis are all enshrined in the Pro Football Hall of Fame in Canton, Ohio, as is the coach who brought them to Cleveland. The team finished its premiere season with a 12-2 record and drew an average of more than 48,000 fans for each Stadium game. The Browns completed their season on December 22 by earning the AAFC crown with a 14-9 victory over the New York Yankees in front of 40,169 at Municipal Stadium.

The Browns captured the AAFC championships the next two years, going 12-1-1 in 1947 and 14-0 in 1948. In some ways, however, the absolute dominance of the Browns brought some unfavorable results. Cleveland's football team was so good that the AAFC never developed the kind of competitive balance that would make the league truly successful. Attendance throughout the AAFC consequently began to drop. Even in Cleveland it happened. In 1949 the Browns' draw slipped to 189,604, a disappointing 31,000 average despite a 9-1-2 record and another championship.

Because of the weakening financial situation in the AAFC, league officials discussed merger with their NFL counterparts. In December 1949, they agreed that the three most successful members of the AAFC, Cleveland, Baltimore, and San Francisco, would be accepted into the NFL for the 1950 season. The remainder of the AAFC disbanded.

That 1950 season was a heady one for the Browns and their fans. The NFL establishment had disparaged the Browns' domination of the AAFC as an "amateur" accomplishment. Little, if any, credit was given to the Cleveland team and its four consecutive AAFC titles. The team felt that it had something to prove. Cleveland's civic pride was at stake as well. The NFL schedule makers decided to give the

The 1950 Browns, in their first year in the NFL, won the league championship, ending all doubts about just how good the team from the "amateur" AAFC really was. (Cleveland Browns photo, Jim Toman collection)

Browns a real test in their first game. They were given the task of playing the NFL champion Philadelphia Eagles in Philadelphia.

In the team's already proud tradition, the Browns began their NFL career as they had begun their AAFC league play. Not only did the Browns win, but they romped over their opposition, handily defeating the Eagles, 35-10. Continuing that early success, they went on to compile a more-than-respectable 10-2 record. At the end of the season, they were tied for the American Conference lead with the New York Giants, and so a playoff game was scheduled. The Browns won 8-3 on the strength of two Lou Groza field goals and a safety and advanced to the final round. The NFL championship game was scheduled for Christmas Eve in Cleveland Stadium. The Browns' opponents were the Los Angeles Rams. Not only was it a game to determine the best team in professional football, but it was also a chance for Clevelanders to gain a measure of revenge against the Rams and their owner Dan Reeves for having abandoned the city five years earlier.

Although a crowd of only 29,751 went to the Stadium in the sub-freezing temperatures and swirling snow, those fans in attendance witnessed a game worthy of greatness. An offensive show all the way, the Rams gained 418 yards to the Browns' 414. At halftime, the Rams were leading, 14-13. The Browns opened the second half with a score to go ahead, 20-14, but Los Angeles scored twice more in the third quarter to take a 28-20 lead into the final period. Otto Graham, who would complete 22 of 33 passes for 298 yards and rush for another 99 yards by the end of the contest, then engineered a 65-yard scoring drive to narrow the score to 28-27. Then, with two minutes left and trailing by one point, the Browns took possession of the ball and began to march down the field. With 20 seconds left on the clock and the ball on the 16-yard line, Lou "the Toe" Groza split the uprights, giving the Browns a 30-28 victory. The Cleveland Browns had garnered the NFL championship in their first season in the league. The fans in attendance witnessed one of the proudest and most memorable moments in Cleveland sports history. Not only did the Browns silence their critics against all odds, they proved to Cleveland, the nation, and the NFL that they were here to stay.

As the Browns developed into league mainstays and continued their championship-caliber play, fans were treated to many exciting moments. One came on November 15, 1953, in a game at the Stadium against the San Francisco 49ers. On hand for the contest was the then-largest crowd ever to see the Browns play, 80,698. In a pre-season game at San Francisco back in August, the Browns had defeated their old AAFC rivals, 20-7. During the game, they had sent 49ers' quarterback Y.A. Tittle to the sidelines with an injury. When the 49ers arrived in Cleveland for the regular season rematch, they were determined to show they could beat the Browns. A hard-fought contest, it was full of the extraordinary heroics and tales that make the sport so popular.

In the second quarter of the game, Otto Graham, unable to find an open receiver, scrambled and headed up field for a 19-yard sprint toward the sidelines. After he crossed the bounds marker, though, San Francisco middle guard Art Michalik threw an elbow, opening a severe gash in Graham's mouth and prompting a bench-clearing brawl. Graham was forced to leave the game.

The Browns' quarterback retired to the locker room, where he received fifteen stitches. At halftime, the 49ers were winning, 10-7, and Cleveland fans were glum about the Browns' prospects for victory. As the brown and orange took the field in the second half, however, one of those running onto the field was Number 14. To the crowd's amazement, Graham was back in the game and ready to go. Not only did he play the entire second half, but he completed nine of ten passes, with two going for touchdowns, and led the team to a 23-21 win. Many who saw the contest remember the quarterback's heroics as their single most memorable moment in Cleveland Municipal Stadium.

Besides being an unforgettable memory, the game also led to a lasting fixture in professional football. The injury sustained by Graham actually prompted Paul Brown to fit a simple plastic bar on his quarterback's helmet to help protect him from further injury. The idea was soon adopted by other teams and has since been modified for players of various positions. Thus, the first face mask on a helmet in the NFL was created.

One of the greatest moments in Browns' history came in the 1950 Championship against the Los Angeles (formerly Cleveland) Rams. Here Lou Groza kicks the winning field goal with just 20 seconds remaining on the clock. (Cleveland Public Library collection)

One of the early stars of the Browns was Dante Lavelli, an exciting receiver for many years. (Browns News Illustrated collection)

Otto Graham led the early Browns' squads from the quarterback position. Here number 14 is being protected by Frank Gatski, number 52. Both were destined for the Football Hall of Fame. (Browns News Illustrated collection)

Just before the 1953 season opened, Art McBride sold the team for $600,000 to a syndicate headed by Dave Jones. At the time, it was the most money ever paid for a football team. Despite the change of ownership, the Browns continued their winning ways. That year, for the fourth consecutive time, they captured the Eastern Conference title and made it to the championship game. Unfortunately, for the third straight year, they lost in the NFL championship round. Los Angeles had exacted revenge in 1951 by beating the Browns, 24-17; Detroit then won, 17-7, in 1952 at Municipal Stadium, and again in 1953 in Detroit by a 17-16 count. The Browns earned two more NFL crowns in 1954 and 1955, though. They finally beat the Lions in front of 43,827 at the Stadium, 56-10, in 1954 and then defeated the Rams in Los Angeles in 1955 by a score of 38-14.

A new era began for the Browns in 1957, when Jim Brown joined the team. For nine years his running electrified the crowds, who came to the Stadium in ever-increasing numbers. Brown rewrote much of the record book and capped a brilliant career with his 1971 induction to the Hall of Fame. (Browns News Illustrated collection)

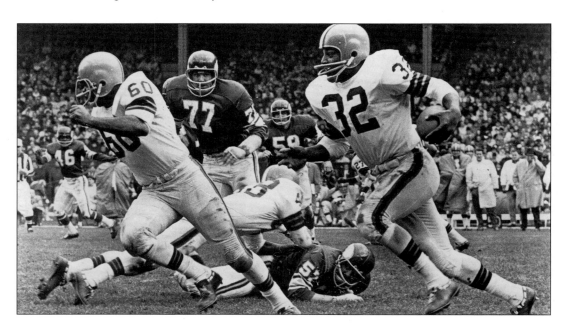

The Cleveland Browns–A Storied Tradition

In just a short time, the Cleveland Browns left no doubt about their ability to play in the NFL. In each of their first six years in the league the team won the conference title. In three of those years they captured the NFL championship. In doing so, the Browns compiled a 58-13-1 overall record. Including their AAFC years, the Cleveland Browns' record was even more spectacular: 105-17-4, with seven (four AAFC and three NFL) championships to their credit. The team had achieved a winning record that no squad before had been able even to approach. With such success, the early popularity of the Browns with Cleveland fans had matured into a love affair.

Inevitably, those heady days came to an end. The 1956 Browns, hampered by the loss of Otto Graham who had retired at the end of the previous season, slipped to a 5-7 record. It was their first losing season. Yet, even the disappointment helped the Browns in the long run. Their record allowed the Browns to draft a player from Syracuse University who was to emerge as perhaps the greatest running back ever to play the game. He would rewrite the record books and bring new excitement to the Cleveland football scene.

In his 1957 rookie season, Jim Brown immediately captivated Browns' fans with his power and skill. At Municipal Stadium on November 24, he ran for 237 yards against the Los Angeles Rams, setting a new league rushing record. His presence helped return Cleveland to its winning ways. In 1957 his running guided the Browns to a 9-2-1 record and another NFL championship game, in which unfortunately they were handily defeated by Detroit, 59-14. The following year the

Art Modell became the Browns' owner in 1961. His tenure as president and owner of the Browns proved to be a stormy one. Here he shows his feelings following a loss to the arch-rival Pittsburgh Steelers. (Cleveland Press Collection of the Cleveland State University Archives)

Browns lost in the playoffs after earning a 9-3 record. Jim Brown added excitement, because he was always a threat for a big gainer. The potential for game-breaking plays paid off for the franchise at the box office as well, lifting Browns' attendance over the 300,000 mark for the first time since 1948. By the time Jim Brown retired after the 1965 season, season attendance had edged past the half-million mark, most likely due in large part to the fullback's electrifying style of play.

In both 1959 and 1960, the Browns continued to win but failed to reach post-season play. The start of the new decade led to the beginning of a new era for the Cleveland Browns, one that would have a lasting effect for the franchise and its fans. On March 21, 1961, New York advertising executive Arthur B. Modell bought the team for $3,925,000, more than six times the 1953 price, the second time in its history the Browns had changed ownership. While Modell described his purchase of the club as a "dream-come-true," his first few years as owner would prove difficult—as would the last few.

The Browns went 8-5-1 in 1961 and finished in third place. At the end of the season, some players began to express their discontent with the club. Jim Brown made it known that he thought the team was overworking him, and quarterback Milt

Plum complained of low morale. Plum soon found himself traded to Detroit for Jim Ninowski. Shortly following Plum's departure, the Browns traded popular running back (and future Hall-of-Famer) Bobby Mitchell to Washington for the first pick in the 1962 draft. Cleveland selected Ernie Davis, a running back from Syracuse University who had captured the 1961 Heisman Trophy.

While these developments made fans nervous, Modell introduced some innovations that proved popular. On August 18, 1962, as part of pre-season play, Municipal Stadium hosted the first-ever pro football doubleheader. A crowd of 77,683, the largest pre-season attendance for a game in Cleveland, turned out to see a 35-24 Detroit win over Dallas in the first game. In the nightcap, fans saw the Browns romp over the Pittsburgh Steelers, 33-10. Because of the initial success, the club held an annual pre-season doubleheader for the next ten years.

The novel doubleheader, though, may have been the highlight of the 1962 campaign, as the Browns' record slipped to 7-6-1. The Ninowski trade had proved a bust; he broke his collarbone, and the team was forced to go with back-up quarterback Frank Ryan. Soon, more grave news hit the Browns. Medical tests revealed that Ernie Davis, from whom so much was expected, could not play because of leukemia. Forced to sit on the sidelines and undergo medical treatment, the running back never played a game for the Browns.

To add to the despair, Modell delivered one of the most shocking announcements in Cleveland sports history. On January 9, 1963, the Browns' owner dismissed Paul Brown, who had directed the team for 17 years. In that time span, Brown's teams went 52-4-3 in the AAFC, winning all the championships in that league, and 115-49-6 in the NFL, winning three NFL crowns. His career totals were overwhelming: a record of 167-53-9 (a .729 winning percentage), 11 appearances in championship games, and seven league crowns.

Modell had viewed the more recent mediocre seasons and signs of player discontent with concern, and felt it was time for a change. The owner, not willing to publicly criticize the coach, would only say that he believed his action was "in the best interests of the Cleveland Browns." Nevertheless, fan reaction was one of outrage. Many could not understand why the hallmark of the organization and the

The 1964 Browns won the NFL Championship, culminating their season with a surprising 27-0 triumph over the Baltimore Colts in a frigid Cleveland Stadium. (Cleveland Browns photo)

person who established the Browns as a dominant force in the NFL would be released. Modell named assistant coach Blanton Collier as Brown's replacement.

More shocking news followed for the Browns' faithful in 1963. Sixth-round draft choice Tom Bloom was killed in an auto accident early in 1963. Then, Ernie Davis lost his battle to leukemia in May 1963. Two weeks later, third-year defensive back Don Fleming was accidentally electrocuted while working on a summer job.

The character of the team prevailed through the turbulent times, however. Under Collier's direction and different style of leadership, the dominating running of Jim Brown (who rushed for 1,863 yards in 1963), and the maturing arm of Frank Ryan (who threw 25 touchdown passes), the brown and orange rebounded to a 10-4 record. Although they fell short of the conference title by one game, the team seemed again to be on the rise.

Throughout 1964 the Browns continued their ascendency to the top of the

Gary Collins, a Browns' mainstay of the 1960s and a star of the 1964 championship game, often provided much excitement for fans. (Browns News Illustrated collection)

NFL, and they were not to be denied. Frank Ryan had another fine year, aided by strong performances from receivers Paul Warfield and Gary Collins. Jim Brown and Ernie Green provided more offensive muscle from the backfield. On defense, Vince Costello, Ross Fichtner, Galen Fiss, Bill Glass, Jim Kanicki, and Dick Modzeleski led the team with their power and skill. The race for the conference title proved to be a tight one, but the Browns handily shook off the challenging New York Giants, 52-20, to win the Eastern Conference title. The victory set up a championship match with Johnny Unitas and the high-powered Baltimore Colts at Municipal Stadium. Few experts expected the Browns to seriously challenge the Colts.

One of the greatest games in Cleveland Browns' history took place on December 27, 1964, a cold and blustery day. That day, 79,544 braved the elements to cheer on the Browns. Most of the rest of Greater Cleveland sat glued by their radios. At the end of the first half, however, no blood had been drawn in the evenly fought contest; the two teams entered their locker rooms with a scoreless tie. Then in the third quarter, veteran place kicker Lou Groza put the game's first points on the board with a 43-yard field goal. Suddenly, as if Groza's feat was the spark, the Frank Ryan-Gary Collins tandem sprung into action. Following the field goal, the two hooked up for three superbly-executed touchdown passes, and were assisted by three Groza extra points and another field goal. The Stadium crowd went wild with excitement, sensing the NFL Championship which had eluded their team for nine years. At the end of the game, the Cleveland Browns pulled out the miracle that virtually nobody had predicted. They had shut out the mighty Colts, 27-0, and in so doing held the vaunted Baltimore offense to 181 yards' total offense. The Browns had gained their fourth NFL title (the city's sixth), and did it in style. The 1964 Browns were also champs at the turnstiles, for the first time averaging more than 70,000 fans per contest and setting in motion a decade-long Browns' attendance boom.

In 1965 the Browns again returned to the championship game, but this time losing 23-12 to the Packers in the snow and mud at Lambeau Field. It was the last game for Jim Brown, who retired after nine seasons with the Cleveland Browns. During his career, he led the league in rushing eight times, gained 12,312 total yards (which stood as a record until Walter Payton broke it in 1984), and finished his career with a 5.2-yard per carry average, still the best among running backs in NFL history. He also scored 126 touchdowns–106 rushing and 20 receiving–in 118 games. In his honor, the team retired his number 32 (also retired are Graham's 14, Groza's 76, Ernie Davis' 45, and Don Fleming's 46). Only six years after he retired he was elected into the Hall of Fame.

Throughout the 1960s, the Browns continued their winning tradition, yet they never again managed to make it to the final round of the championship. In June 1966, the NFL and the rival American Football League agreed to merge and create the first Super Bowl (not so named until two years later). That season, the Kansas City Chiefs and Green Bay Packers competed in the season's final contest. To accommodate the new arrangement, officials restructured the NFL into divisions and conferences. The Browns were assigned to the Century Division of the Eastern Conference. The team won its division in 1967 and earned trips to the conference championships in both 1968 and 1969.

After a slow 2-3 start in 1968, the Browns won eight games in a row, finishing the regular season at 10-4 and capturing the division title for the second consecutive year. The Browns played the Eastern Conference championship game against Dallas at the Stadium on December 21, and beat the visitors, 31-20. Cleveland's victory meant another showdown with Baltimore for the league title one week later, also to be held on the lakefront. Fans were so excited about the game that 15,000 endured for hours a drenching rain to buy tickets. The Colts, however, frustrated the Browns' hopes for their first invitation to the Super Bowl and avenged their 1964 loss. As 80,628 Stadium stunned fans looked on, the Colts turned back Bill Nelsen, Leroy Kelly, Milt Morin, Paul Warfield, and company, 34-0. It was only the third time in Browns' history that the team had been shut out.

In 1969, the Browns again made it to the league championship game but lost to the Minnesota Vikings at Bloomington, 27-7. The Browns finished with only one championship in the 1960s, but their 101-46-5 record and five trips to the post-season in that span showed they were consistently one of the best teams in the NFL.

In 1970 the NFL witnessed a few changes. The merger between the NFL and AFL was finalized that year. The Browns, along with Baltimore and Pittsburgh, moved to the American Conference, and they were assigned to the new Central Division. Also, the league, capitalizing on the popularity of professional football, arranged an agreement with ABC Television to premiere Monday Night Football. Because a jammed Municipal Stadium was so impressive a backdrop, the league invited Cleveland to host the first telecast. Network hopes for dynamic crowd scenes were fully satisfied for the September 21 game, as 85,703 crushed into the lakefront facility to see their hometown team beat the New York Jets 31-21. It remains the largest crowd ever to see a Browns' contest. Unfortunately for the Browns, the rest of the season was less successful; they finished with a 7-7 record, and at the end of the season, Blanton Collier, afflicted by a hearing loss, retired as head coach. In his eight campaigns at the Browns' helm, he had achieved a successful record of 76-34-2 (a .679 winning percentage).

For the Browns and their fans, the 1970s were to look nothing like the 1960s. Under new head coach Nick Skorich, the Browns reached the playoffs in 1971 but lost in the first round. Despite a fine 10-4 record in 1972, they finished second in the division and did not make it to the playoffs. The 1973 Browns slipped another notch, missing the playoffs and going 7-5-2. For the second time ever in Browns' history, the 1974 Browns posted a losing season, dropping to a dismal 4-10 record. In the 1975 season, Forrest Gregg became the Browns' fourth head coach, but he was unable to improve the Browns' on-field performance; that year, they dipped to their then-worst franchise record of 3-11. The team rebounded to an impressive 9-5 record in 1976, but still finished third in the Central Division. In 1977, the last year of Forrest Gregg's reign, the Browns were 6-8. As the quality on the field dipped, so too did the attendance. The Stadium fan count had peaked in 1969 when 578,360 fans made their way to the lakefront. By 1975, that figure had fallen to 390,440.

While the 1970s represented somewhat of a drought for the Browns, one thing to cheer about was this Joe Jones tackle of Pittsburgh Steelers' quarterback Terry Bradshaw. (Paul Tepley photo)

Browns-Steelers match-ups at the Stadium always brought a full house and provided plenty of drama. Here Jerry Sherk pressures Terry Bradshaw. (Browns News Illustrated collection)

The Browns' return to winning ways was keyed by the quarterbacking of Brian Sipe, who led the team from 1976-1983. He piloted the famous "Kardiac Kids" during the 1980 season and became the holder of many Browns' quarterback records. (Browns News Illustrated collection)

Sam Rutigliano became Art Modell's hand-picked successor to lead the team in 1978. The new coach began to turn around the Browns' fortunes, guiding the team to an 8-8 record in 1978 and a 9-7 record in 1979. More importantly, the brown and orange were playing exciting football again. Often, the game's outcome would be uncertain until the final minutes. The Browns gained a new nickname; they became the "Kardiac Kids." For instance, 12 of the 16 games in 1979 were decided by a touchdown or fewer points; in those tight contests, the Browns were 7-5. Responding to the electrifying style of play, the fans began to return to Municipal Stadium. In 1979, they drew 200,000 more in attendance than they had just four years earlier. Altogether, in the 1970s the Browns put together a mediocre 72-70-2 record.

The 1980s began on a dynamic note for the Browns, and much of the team's success can be attributed to Brian Sipe. Sipe had taken over the reins at quarterback during the first game of the 1976 season after Mike Phipps went down with a separated shoulder. By 1979 Sipe had blossomed into a premier quarterback; that year he threw 28 touchdown passes and set a team record with 3,793 passing yards. In 1980 Sipe surpassed his previous feats. Assisted by the talents of wide receiver Reggie Rucker, running back Mike Pruitt, and tight end Ozzie Newsome, Sipe threw for 4,132 yards, 30 touchdowns–both Browns' records–and completed 61 percent of his passes as he led the team to an 11-5 record and a Central Division title. For his performance, Sipe earned the AFC's "player of the year" award.

The Kardiac Kids operated full-tilt in 1980. The Browns were so exciting that fans responded by going to the lakefront in record numbers. The 1980 season attendance of 620,496 remains the highest season attendance in Cleveland Browns' history. Nine of the 16 games that season were settled only during the final two minutes of play, and 12 were won by margins of one touchdown or less.

Actually, ten games in the 1980 season were decided in the last two minutes of play if one counts the now-infamous playoff game against the Oakland Raiders on January 4, 1981. Temperatures at game time hovered near the zero mark, and the wind-chill factor made the Stadium feel like -30 degrees. In typical fashion, though, 77,655 of Cleveland's hardiest fans turned out for the contest, despite the fact that the game was televised locally. The Browns took possession of the ball with less than two minutes to play, trailing 14-12. In true Kardiac Kid fashion, Sipe led the Browns down the frozen field with precision passing and cool confidence. Forsaking a short field goal attempt on the icy field, Rutigliano called for a pass play: "Red Right 88."

Sipe's intended pass to Ozzie Newsome, however, was intercepted in the end zone by Oakland defender Mike Davis with 49 seconds left on the clock, ending the Browns' "kardiac" season. In the chronicle of near-misses, that final play has come to be remembered simply as "The Pass." It was the first real chance the Browns had of reaching the Super Bowl in nine years, and the abrupt end to the season hit fans hard.

Perhaps haunted by being so close, the 1981 Browns fell to 5-11, and in 1982 the NFL season was nearly wiped out by a 57-day strike. That season they went 4-5. The 1983 Browns climbed above .500 with a 9-7 record, but despite another fine year by Sipe (who passed for 3,566 yards and 28 touchdowns), the brown and orange fell short of the playoffs. It was to be Sipe's final year with the team. He signed a contract to play for the New Jersey Generals of the newly formed United States Football League. He left the team holding many all-time Browns' records for passing, including most yards, attempts, completions, touchdowns, interceptions, and career 300-yard games. Without him, the Browns lost seven of their first eight games in 1984, prompting Modell to replace his friend Sam Rutigliano, who had directed the team to a record of 47-50 in seven-and-a-half seasons, with Marty Schottenheimer.

In 1985, the Browns' fortunes began to look bright again. That year, Schottenheimer had a new quarterback with whom to work. The Browns had acquired Bernie Kosar in the 1985 supplemental draft. Kosar, a native of the Youngstown area and a standout at the University of Miami, had made it clear that he wanted to play for Cleveland. He told the media that it had been a boyhood dream to play for the brown and orange. With such explicit interest in the Browns and northeast Ohio, Kosar became instantly popular with many Cleveland fans. With Kosar at the helm, Kevin Mack and Earnest Byner in the backfield, and Hanford Dixon and Frank Minnifield (who nicknamed the defense the "Dawgs" and inspired creation of bleacher section "Dawg Pound," which became the signature image of Browns' fans) leading the defense, the Browns began a five-year string of winning seasons and post-season play.

Although the 1985 Browns finished 8-8, they earned a Central Division crown and a trip to the post-season. During Kosar's rookie season, Mack and Byner each gained more than 1,000 yards rushing, becoming only the third tandem in NFL history to accomplish such a feat. The Browns lost to the Miami Dolphins in the playoffs despite being ahead at one point, 21-3.

The team's talent was to keep them on the winning track, and exciting post-season appearances continued into the

Though criticized for his side-arm deliveries, Bernie Kosar became a fan favorite in Cleveland. In five of his first six seasons, he led the team into post-season play. (Browns News Illustrated collection)

following seasons, but ultimate victory eluded the team each year as it did in 1985. In 1986, after the Browns earned a 12-4 regular-season record, the first playoff game in Cleveland since the 1981 Oakland loss took place on January 3, 1987, against the New York Jets in front of 78,106 fans. In a game that many regard as perhaps one of the greatest comebacks in NFL history and one of the most memorable games in Stadium history, the young Kosar guided the Browns to tie the Jets, 20-20, with seven seconds left in the game, after being down 20-10 with just over four minutes remaining. Keeping the fans on the edges of their seats, the game went into double overtime—the only playoff game ever to do so—before the Browns prevailed, 23-20. Kosar's 489 yards passing that day still stands as a Browns' single-game record as well as an NFL playoff record.

The victory brought the Denver Broncos to town for the American Conference championship game the following week, a game which put Browns' fans on an emotional roller coaster ride. Following an exciting touchdown pass to receiver Brian Brennan to put the Browns ahead by a touchdown, Denver had the ball on its own two-yard line with just four minutes remaining. Cleveland fans felt victory was in hand. But it was not to be. Denver quarterback John Elway engineered what came to be referred to simply as "The Drive." The Broncos marched down the field and tied the game with 37 seconds left in regulation. In overtime, Denver's barefoot place

The closest moment the Browns ever had to reaching the Super Bowl came when receiver Brian Brennan caught a pass from Kosar late in the fourth quarter of the AFC championship game against Denver in the Stadium. It put the Browns up by a touchdown. (Browns News Illustrated collection)

kicker Rich Karlis booted the winning field goal, and the Browns were once again denied their first Super Bowl appearance. Cleveland Stadium fell ghostly quiet as the 75,993 stunned fans filed out in disappointment.

Following the 1987 season which was disrupted by a players' strike and three games played by a replacement team, the Browns again made it to the playoffs with a 10-5 record. In the first post-season game, Cleveland defeated the Indianapolis Colts at the Stadium, 38-21, setting up a championship game rematch against the Broncos in Denver's Mile High Stadium. After being down, 28-10, Kosar and Byner led a Browns' comeback to within a touchdown, 38-31. In the Browns' final drive, with the ball at Denver's eight-yard line and the Browns threatening to tie the score, Earnest Byner fumbled the ball at the goal line, and it was recovered by the Broncos. Cleveland lost another heartbreaker, 38-33. "The Fumble" joined "The Drive" and "The Pass" in the continuing saga of a dream denied.

In 1988 the Browns again made it to the playoffs, this time as a wild-card team; in another nail-biter, the Houston Oilers eliminated the Browns from the title chase, 24-23. That game proved to be Marty Schottenheimer's last, as he and Modell disagreed over the future of the team. Schottenheimer had led the team for

The Cleveland Browns—A Storied Tradition

Tight end Ozzie Newsome became a Cleveland favorite during the 1980s. The sure-handed receiver holds the Browns' record for most receptions in a game, in a season, and in a career. (Browns News Illustrated collection)

four-and-a-half seasons, compiling a strong 46-31 record. He was the most successful Browns' coach since Blanton Collier, taking the Browns into post-season play each year he was at the helm.

Bud Carson became the Browns' next head coach, and the 1989 squad returned to its winning ways, earning a 9-6-1 record and another Central Division title. In the first playoff game, the Browns hosted the Buffalo Bills on January 6, 1990, in front of 77,706 fans. The contest was not decided until the final seconds, when veteran linebacker Clay Matthews intercepted a Jim Kelly pass at the goal line to preserve a 34-30 win. The victory set up yet another rematch with Denver in the AFC championship game—the third in four years. The game, played in Denver, had a familiar ending; despite an exciting third quarter, the Broncos defeated the Browns, 37-21. The loss at Mile High Stadium brought a decade of dramatic Cleveland football to an end. Despite never having reached the Super Bowl, the Browns attained a record of 83-68-1, made it to the playoffs seven times, and returned professional football in Cleveland to its winning and thrilling ways.

Though Marty Schottenheimer guided the Browns to post-season appearances in each of his four seasons as full-time head coach, his disagreements with Modell led to his departure after the 1988 season. (Browns News Illustrated collection)

Unfortunately, the 1990s began on a much more grim note. The team, which began the rebuilding process after the championship loss in Denver, achieved its worst record in franchise history. Not only did the Browns stumble to a 3-13 record, many of the losses were embarrassing. They gave up an average of 28 points a game in their losses and were shut out twice. By mid-season, Carson was replaced by offensive coordinator Jim Shofner. The losses, however, continued and attendance plummeted. For the first time since 1981, the Browns became too painful to watch.

Despite winter's worst, Cleveland fans were never deterred from cheering on the Browns at their lakefront home. Here Matt Stover attempts a field goal against the Houston Oilers. (Browns News Illustrated collection)

Many faithful Browns' fans, however, were disposed to see the 1990 season as an aberration. With the 1991 appointment of Bill Belichick as head coach, the ninth in team history, hopes were rekindled for a return to winning ways. Reassuring the media of his confidence in Belichick, Modell said he would not hire another head coach—either Belichick got the job done, or Modell would leave professional football. Yet, in the quest to return the Browns to dominance, the Belichick era would forever alter the future of the Cleveland Browns.

From the start, Belichick was not a popular head coach. His tight-lipped approach and reserved personality did not seem to mesh well with fans or the media. His teams made slow but steady strides, however. In 1991, the Browns improved to 6-10, and in 1992, they achieved a 7-9 record. Following the 1992 campaign, Modell uttered words that in a few short years would again ring in the ears of Browns' fans. In a press conference assessing the progress of the team under Belichick's direction, Modell flatly told those gathered that he was so confident of Belichick's future with the Browns that if they didn't get the job done by 1995, he would get out of football and leave Cleveland. "I will not," Modell said, "hire another coach."

The 1993 Browns began the season on a promising note, as they started the season 5-2 and created some excitement. But injuries to key players took their toll, and their impact on a still youthful team resulted in a string of defeats.

Perhaps the beginning of the end between Cleveland fans and the Browns' front office occurred in the middle of that 1993 season. Two important moments earlier in the season might have forecast future events. In a Monday night game at the Stadium against the powerful San Francisco 49ers which the Browns won, Kosar threw a picture-perfect pass to receiver Michael Jackson, who stretched out fully and caught it in the end zone in front of the Dawg Pound. In the midst of wild celebration, Kosar returned to the sidelines, only to be seemingly rebuked by Belichick. Evidently, the quarterback had changed the play, and the head coach was angry. Six games later in a contest against Denver at the Stadium, Kosar was seen drawing up a play in the dirt with Michael Jackson. The improvised play resulted in a 33-yard touchdown, but again, Belichick appeared furious with his quarterback for bucking the plans.

The game against Denver proved to be Kosar's last in the brown and orange, as the Browns released the popular quarterback the next day. Belichick referred to Kosar's "diminishing skills." Modell sat silently. The controversial announcement, coming midway through the season, stunned loyal Browns' fans. Callers on radio talk shows and on television reacted angrily to the way in which Kosar was let go; many believed that Kosar, who had come to Cleveland because he wanted to play for the Browns, deserved a more appropriate send-off. Fans now perceived the Browns' front office as insensitive.

The fans were frustrated, and attendance dipped for the last three home games. The finale drew only 39,860 fans, the lowest attendance for a regular season contest since 1978. The season ended with the Browns again missing the .500 mark, another 7-9 record.

In 1994, though, the Browns began to play the way Belichick had envisioned. Racing off to a 7-2 start, the brown and orange played well both offensively and defensively. The team finished 11-5, set a new team record for the fewest sacks allowed in a season (14), and it allowed the fewest number of points in the NFL. As a wild card team in the playoffs, the Browns defeated the New England Patriots, 20-13, at the Stadium to force a showdown with the rival Pittsburgh Steelers, which the Browns lost, 29-9. Even with such on-field success, however, the 1994 attendance of 559,582 remained disappointing, as the Browns drew almost 10,000 fewer fans than during 1993. Fans could still be heard talking about Bernie Kosar.

At the start of the 1995 season, many pundits picked the Browns to finally reach the Super Bowl. They were expected to build on their 1994 success, especially with the addition of key free agents such as receiver Andre Rison, running back Lorenzo White, and linebacker Craig Powell. Discussion about Stadium plans, renovations, leases, and rumors of franchise moves, however, would soon prove distracting for the Browns and their fans.

Problems and signs of discontent slowly began to tarnish the gleam of hope for the Browns. Rison's expensive contract provoked other players to voice dissatisfaction with their contracts, forcing the Browns to renegotiate with many players. Former Browns' players who signed with other teams before the 1995 season openly criticized the situation in Cleveland. Some players did not like Belichick's style, and there were rumors about his demeaning treatment of players and of deep personal animosities. To add to these problems, fans did not seem as excited about the season; corporations began to cancel Stadium loges, and the home opener drew fewer than 62,000 fans, the lowest first-game total in over 20 years. Certainly, these signs did not portend overwhelming success or enthusiasm.

Webster Slaughter leads the fans in the bleachers in celebration after catching a touchdown pass. The zeal of the "Dawg Pound" was recognized around the league. (Browns News Illustrated collection)

The 1995 Browns started quickly with a 3-1 record, but the team soon found itself on a downward spiral that would be irreversible. Coaches and players feuded openly in the media. Modell expressed concerns about the use of the Browns' backfield, which was loaded with talent but not producing. A quarterback controversy became a focus each week. Some players were not putting forth full effort for a coach they did not like. The Browns began losing games, and critics said they were not playing like contenders.

On November 6, 1995, all of the season's frustration came to a stunning climax. On a hastily erected podium in downtown Baltimore, Art Modell announced he was moving the Cleveland Browns to Baltimore because of financial considerations. He told reporters and fans he "had no choice" because the Browns had been losing millions over the previous few years.

Fan reaction to the announcement was one of outrage. Cleveland Mayor Mike White and supporters spoke openly about "being kicked in the teeth" by Modell and the Browns. A "Save Our Browns" campaign was established to bombard NFL owners with protests over the move. Companies pulled their advertisements from the Stadium, leaving the scoreboard and other parts of the facility looking barren and lifeless. Clevelanders even traveled to nearby Pittsburgh, hoping to rally support for their beloved Browns by wearing orange arm bands.

At the time of Modell's announcement, the Browns' record was 4-4. For the rest of the season, the Browns, distracted by the controversy, continued to lose

This scene accurately depicts the disappointing 1995 season. A downcast Antonio Langham and the paucity of fans tell the story. (Browns News Illustrated collection)

games. Appropriately, their next and last win came in the final home game at Municipal Stadium against the Cincinnati Bengals. In a game where fans came to say farewell to the players and the Stadium which had been the site for 50 years of heart-stopping victories and heart-breaking defeats, the Browns easily defeated their down-state rivals, 26-10. The 55,875 fans who attended counted down the final seconds on the Stadium scoreboard clock. Following the game, Browns' players went to the Dawg Pound and embraced the fans that for so long had embraced them. The love affair that had begun with Paul Brown and continued for so long was left to languish on the frozen turf in an uncertain future.

The final record for the 1995 Browns was a disappointing 5-11. In Belichick's five years as head coach, he guided the Browns to a 37-45 record overall and a .451 winning percentage, the second lowest among Browns' head coaches (of more than one season). The numbers for the decade looked even more grim. During the 1990s, the brown and orange was 40-58.

But Cleveland fans have and will continue to support the Browns. Throughout the Stadium's history, 26,021,893 Browns' fans made their way to the lakefront to cheer on their team. Average attendance for all games, pre-season, regular season, and playoffs, was 63,468. Average regular season attendance was 69,446. In turn, the Browns treated their fans to a total of 248 home field wins, while losing 153, and with 7 games ending as ties. At the Stadium the Browns compiled a .618 winning percentage.

The Stadium is forever gone. With it went the Dawg Pound and the press boxes atop the Stadium from which so many fans heard Nev Chandler's calls. The huge parking lot which once housed numerous tailgate parties and post-game celebrations has been replaced by the Rock 'n Roll Hall of Fame and Museum and the Great Lakes Science Center. Gone are the wrap-around upper decks, the girders supporting the roof, the frozen turf, and the dugouts from which Browns' players emerged onto the field to a rising roar from rabid fans. What remains are the memories of victories, defeats, and heroics, deeply etched in the minds of all who rooted for their team.

Under an agreement negotiated between the City of Cleveland and the NFL, the Browns will play in Cleveland again come 1999. It will be in a different stadium. It will be with a different owner. If history is any judge, the same enthusiasm that supported the team throughout its storied history will be waiting for them.

BROWNS' HEAD COACHES

COACH	YEARS	WON-LOSS RECORD (Winning Percentage)
Paul Brown	1946-1962	167-53-8 (.759)
Blanton Collier	1963-1970	79-38-2 (.675)
Nick Skorich	1971-1974	30-26-2 (.536)
Forrest Gregg	1975-1977	18-23 (.439)
Dick Modzelewski	1977	0-1 (.000)
Sam Rutigliano	1978-1984	47-51 (.480)
Marty Schottenheimer	1984-1988	46-31 (.597)
Bud Carson	1989-1990	12-14-1 (.463)
Jim Shofner	1990	1-7 (.125)
Bill Belichick	1991-1995	37-45 (.451)

BROWNS' HOME ATTENDANCE
AND WON-LOSS RECORDS

SEASON	REGULAR SEASON HOME W-L	REGULAR SEASON OVERALL W-L	PRE-SEASON HOME ATTENDANCE	REGULAR SEASON HOME ATTENDANCE	PLAYOFF HOME ATTENDANCE
1946	6-1	12-2		339,962	40,469
1947	6-1	12-1-1		392,760	
1948	7-0	14-0		318,619	22,981
1949	5-0-1	9-1-2	31,157	189,604	39,820
1950	5-1	10-2	51,076	200,319	62,805
1951	6-0	11-1	38,851	231,414	
1952	4-2	8-4	37,976	240,204	50,934
1953	6-0	11-1	22,336	274,671	
1954	5-1	9-3	17,631	183,476	43,827
1955	5-1	9-2-1	29,581	251,444	
1956	1-5	5-7	15,456	221,648	
1957	6-0	9-2-1	34,369	324,165	
1958	4-2	9-3	35,343	370,781	
1959	3-3	7-5	25,316	338,380	
1960	4-2	8-3-1	25,911	337,972	
1961	4-3	8-5-1	41,374	426,886	
1962	4-2-1	7-6-1	77,683	422,043	
1963	5-2	10-4	83,218	487,430	
1964	5-1-1	10-3-1	83,736	549,334	79,544
1965	5-2	11-3	83,118	557,283	
1966	5-2	9-5	83,418	544,250	
1967	6-1	9-5	84,236	544,807	
1968	5-2	10-4	84,918	527,107	162,125
1969	5-1-1	10-3-1	85,532	578,360	
1970	4-3	7-7	83,043	567,377	
1971	4-3	9-5	82,710	541,505	74,082
1972	4-3	10-4	70,583	528,591	
1973	5-1-1	7-5-2	129,795	490,406	
1974	3-4	4-10	68,536	424,412	
1975	3-4	3-11	99,265	390,440	

BROWNS' HOME ATTENDANCE
AND WON-LOSS RECORDS

SEASON	REGULAR SEASON HOME W-L	REGULAR SEASON OVERALL W-L	PRE-SEASON HOME ATTENDANCE	REGULAR SEASON HOME ATTENDANCE	PLAYOFF HOME ATTENDANCE
1976	6-1	9-5	80,352	472,602	
1977	2-5	6-8	100,460	480,805	
1978	5-3	8-8	61,981	510,046	
1979	5-3	9-7	43,056	593,821	
1980	6-2	11-5	54,986	620,496	77,655
1981	3-5	5-11	120,105	601,725	
1982	2-2	4-5	60,794	251,314	
1983	6-2	9-7	61,844	564,639	
1984	2-6	5-11	47,381	458,433	
1985	5-3	8-8	91,162	535,752	
1986	6-2	12-4	58,982	583,739	158,021
1987	5-2	10-5	78,650	492,939	75,586
1988	6-2	10-6	149,194	615,545	74,977
1989	5-2-1	9-6-1	134,425	613,415	77,706
1990	2-6	3-13	123,433	568,093	
1991	3-5	6-10	119,198	571,752	
1992	4-4	7-9	115,321	560,417	
1993	4-4	7-9	51,361	568,474	
1994	6-2	11-5	99,057	559,582	77,452
1995	3-5	4-12	90,001	566,894	

Note: In addition to 408 regular season games played at Cleveland Stadium, the Browns also played 64 pre-season and 19 post-season games there.

THE FINAL CURTAIN COMES DOWN

8

The Cleveland Browns played their last home game at Cleveland Municipal Stadium on December 18, 1995. The crowd was subdued, and the Stadium looked somber. A coat of black paint had been applied to all of the advertising on the scoreboards and along the concourses. Advertisers had demanded the cover-up as a sign of their solidarity with the feelings of the fans, outraged at the Browns' owner. The fans that day were not there so much to watch a football game as they were to witness the end of an era in the city.

Thus, despite this final home victory, the mood of the fans was hardly celebratory. They were losing their beloved football team to Baltimore, and team president Art Modell was the focal point for the their continuing sense of betrayal. Following the game, the media made much of the fans' still boiling anger. Some fans had demonstrated their resentment by tearing loose some chairs from the grandstand and smashing some of the plank seating in the bleachers. The Stadium maintenance crew estimated that 8,000 seats had been damaged. But unlike the typical routine following other games, this time the damage would not be repaired.

More than the normal winter clouds were hanging over the Stadium in December 1995. While the citizens of Cuyahoga County had authorized the final piece in public funding for renovating the Stadium, Modell's decision to move the team to Baltimore for the 1996 season had made renovation pointless. It made no sense to spend $172 million to renovate a facility that had no permanent tenant.

The fact, however, that the Browns had a lease with Stadium Corporation to play their home games there through the 1998 season, gave the City of Cleveland a legal leverage point. Even though the Browns and Stadium Corporation (both Modell-controlled businesses) had amicably agreed in late October 1995 to cancel the lease, the City questioned the validity of that solution. Soon lawyers for the City were busy preparing their brief to the court seeking injunctive relief against the premature termination of the Browns' stay in Cleveland. The City's arguments in round one prevailed, and on November 24, 1995, Judge Kenneth Callahan of the Cuyahoga County Common Pleas Court held that a full hearing would have to be scheduled to decide the merits of the case.

While the parties awaited the court date and the legal arguments were being daily aired in the media, the involved parties, the Browns, the City of Cleveland, and the National Football League, recognized that an out-of-court settlement was the only reasonable option. To force the Browns to play their home games in Cleveland in 1996–no doubt the team would have been reconstituted as a "low-priced model"– before a largely empty Stadium, would not have served the best interests of competitive football in the league. Nor would it have satisfied the loyal fans of Cleveland who longed for a team they could love, a team like those of the not too distant past led by popular stars such as Brian Sipe and Bernie Kosar.

And so behind-doors negotiations got underway to find a so-called "win-win" solution. While the public rhetoric continued to flow unabated, negotiators struggled in a more business-oriented fashion during December and January to reach a final agreement. Those terms were eventually ironed out, and they were announced in a meeting in Chicago on February 8, 1996.

Art Modell would be allowed to take his team to Baltimore and begin playing there in 1996. They would need a new name and new colors, however, for the "Browns," the "orange and brown," and the records established over 50 years of Cleveland football were being reserved for a new Cleveland team which the NFL guaranteed would begin play in 1999. In return for the uncontested right to relocate, Modell agreed to pay the City $11.5 million in compensation for revenues that would be lost in the interim. The City of Cleveland, in turn, agreed to the NFL demand that it tear down the old Stadium and use the money intended for its renovation to build a new facility. To bridge the gap in financing between the $172 million cost of renovating the old Stadium and the $220 million price tag for a new one, the NFL agreed to advance the City as much as $48 million towards construction costs. The loan would eventually be repaid by the next owner of the Browns' franchise.

The agreement fulfilled Modell's wish to leave Cleveland. The City was going to retain its place as an NFL mainstay. The NFL was able to minimize a public relations nightmare. Win. Win. Win.

There was one loser, though. Cleveland Municipal Stadium, apparently rescued by the recent vote of the people, was sacrificed to meet the expectations of the NFL. The legend on the lake would have to make way for a newer, brighter, cleaner facility. The Stadium would be razed just as soon as possible to make way for the new facility.

Cleveland Mayor Michael White had agreed in the negotiations to replace the old Stadium with a new open-air facility on the same site. Not everyone agreed with that decision. Some campaigned that the new facility should be a dome so that it would be more versatile. Estimates, however, put the price of a domed building at some $80 million more than for the open-air facility, and so that idea was dropped. Some members of Cleveland City Council favored building the new stadium closer to the Gateway Complex, on a site owned by the Norfolk Southern Railroad. This would have allowed the lakefront site to be developed with other tourist attractions, such as the aquarium for which further planning had been postponed. A study panel, however, on April 23, 1996, came out in favor of the lakefront site. To keep the new stadium project on schedule, this would mean that demolition on the old Stadium would have to begin by the end of the year.

As the winter of Cleveland's discontent gave way to spring, the Stadium stood largely abandoned. Cleveland Stadium Corporation handed responsibility for the facility back to the City, and by April 1, 1996, the company's offices in Tower B

THE CITY OF CLEVELAND, THE BROWNS
AND THE NFL THANK YOU FOR ATTENDING
"THE FINAL PLAY".

were largely empty. The only signs of life came from the Stadium Restaurant in Tower A, which under new management continued to serve its lunch-time patrons. The restaurant remained open until September 20, 1996.

By summer, the interior of the Stadium showed the signs of subtle but unmistakable neglect. The field no longer received the loving care of a professional groundskeeper. Only intermittently cut and watered, the grass was patchy, and the scars of the last football season were plainly visible.

The red brick track area sported weeds, which also managed to grow in cracks in various areas of the grandstand. Here and there seats were missing. A layer of dust covered everything. And spider webs were laced everywhere, from the rooftop boxes to the loge walkways to the tunnels connecting the dugouts to the locker rooms. Up close, the old Stadium's wrinkles were all too apparent. And yet, if one looked across the field, at the sweep of the grandstand, the old girl still looked mighty fine indeed. It was hard to believe that her days were numbered.

Yet even as the final countdown began, the City decided to host one last weekend at Cleveland Municipal Stadium. The Final Play on September 21-22 gave fans a last chance to see the venerable old facility, and perhaps to buy a piece of history. On September 24 parties interested in bidding on various Stadium artifacts, from turnstiles to trash containers, attended an auction.

Over the next weeks, the seats and others bits and pieces of the Stadium that had been purchased

There is no time left on the clock for the City of Cleveland's farewell to the Stadium. Approximately 100,000 came to visit the Stadium one last time during the two-day event. (Greg Deegan photo)

By October 1996, workers had removed the seats that fans had ordered as souvenirs. Remnants litter the field. (Greg Deegan photo)

An early November snow storm failed to slow the Stadium demolition schedule. A fence secures the site for the wrecking crews. (Jim Toman photo)

Actual demolition of the Stadium structure began on November 25, 1996. The bleacher section was the first to feel the wrecking ball. (Browns News Illustrated)

were removed from the site, while the City of Cleveland evaluated the bids submitted for the demolition contract. A total of 19 different firms bid for the right to raze the Stadium. Bids ranged from $2.9 to $12.8 million. Only three days after receiving them, on October 18, the City awarded the contract to Demco, Inc. from Orchard Park, New York, the low bidder.

Before the actual work of razing the old structure could begin, however, workers first had to remove asbestos and other contaminants from the building and the roof. Once actual demolition got underway, the debris would be separated.

More than half of the 20,000 cubic yards of concrete from the Stadium would be saved to construct a fishing reef in Lake Erie. Some 10,000 of the yellow bricks would also be saved and sold as souvenirs. The steel and aluminum would be sold to recyclers.

By the third week in November, the preliminary work was completed, and a fence had been erected around the Stadium site. On November 25, 1996, as the mayor and a couple hundred curious onlookers watched, the actual demolition got underway. The bleacher section was the first targeted by the wreckers. Eight hydraulic excavators and two cranes with 10,000-pound wrecking balls were on the site. As the excavators' claws chewed into the brickwork, the wrecking balls fell against steel and concrete. Very quickly huge holes began to appear in the old Dawg Pound.

Another early casualty was the Donald Gray Gardens. Although preservationists and naturalists had hoped the last remnant of the Great Lakes Exposition could be spared, planners said that its 3.5 acres were needed as part of the construction site. Bulldozers made short work of the gardens.

Demolition then worked its way around from the bleachers to the northern section between Gates C and B. First the columns holding up the roof were cut. Then the columns

The Final Curtain Comes Down

By early December 1996, the Stadium's roof began to come off. Demolition proceeded counterclockwise, beginning at Gate C. (Jim Toman photo)

supporting the upper deck followed. When the columns were then yanked free, the roof or deck would collapse. Demolition continued in a counter-clockwise format. Next to go was the section between Gates B and A, facing West Third Street; then came the section between Gates A and D. Finally all that remained standing were the four corner towers. Tower C was the last to fall. It tumbled down during the last week of January 1997. By February 1, all that remained of Cleveland Municipal Stadium were the piles of debris still waiting to be carted from the site and the pilings which had been used to create its foundation. While the old piles were still sound, differences in the footprint of the new stadium would essentially require new piling work. Some of the old, however, will remain in place.

During the ten weeks that demolition was underway, there was a steady stream of slow traffic along the Stadium's perimeter. Frequently cars would pull to the side of the road, and the driver or passenger would jump out to photograph the vanishing scene. Others just drove slowly by. It was hard to imagine how something that always had seemed so substantial could disappear so quickly.

The upper and lower decks soon followed the roof into oblivion. (Jim Toman photo)

Eight hydraulic excavators made short work of the Stadium's superstructure. (Jim Toman photo)

On February 1, 1997, the City of Cleveland gave Stadium souvenir seekers one more chance to buy a piece of history. Ten thousand of the Stadium's bricks went on sale for $10 apiece. The city expected that it would take several days to sell them all. They were all gone in just two days.

In 1993 more than two million fans made their way into Cleveland Stadium to see the Cleveland Indians play their final season there. They did not come to see

By mid-December the outer walls were tumbling down. The former offices of the Stadium Corporation are in the foreground. (Greg Deegan photo)

The Final Curtain Comes Down

By January 1997, only the Stadium's four towers remain. Tower A is in the foreground, Tower B in the background. (Jim Toman photo)

By the end of January, a partial Tower C was all that was still standing. (Jim Toman photo)

a pennant contender, for the Indians that year had not yet gelled as a competitive team. Rather, the people came from a nostalgic sense of connection to a place that would no longer be a baseball park.

In 1996 and 1997, the crowds that flocked to the Final Play, those who bought seats, bricks, or other memorabilia, and those who just drove by one last time, were all demonstrating their affection for Cleveland's wonderful old Stadium. It was wonderful because it was the scene of so many memories, for 65 years so much a part of the fabric of growing up and growing old as a Clevelander.

After so many years of faithful service, Cleveland Municipal Stadium is no more. But the memories are still with us. No bulldozer can take those away.

A January 21, 1997, aerial view of the site is more reminiscent of a lunar crater than of the former home of the Indians and Browns. (David Kachinko photo)

The Final Curtain Comes Down

By February 1997, all that remained of Cleveland Municipal Stadium was a pile of rubble, which was carted away to become a fishing reef in Lake Erie. The Great Lakes Science Center is in the background. (Jim Toman photo)

OWN AN AUTHENTIC PIECE OF CLEVELAND SPORTS HISTORY

As purchaser of the Main Scoreboard prior to the demolition of Cleveland Stadium, Stadium Memories has produced a line of authentic memorabilia to celebrate the history of the "Grand Old Lady."

ONE LIGHT PLAQUE
(#100B)

PERSONALIZED PLAQUE
(#101B)

LIGHTED SCOREBOARD CABINET
(#102B)

ONE LIGHT PLAQUE (#100B) - $49 PLUS TAX/SHIPPING

This 10 by 8 inch almond colored plaque includes an actual section of the "Dawg Pound" scoreboard along with one of the lights used in the board. Engraved on the plaque is our rendition of the "Grand Old Lady." The plaque is designed to be hung on a wall and would make an ideal conversation piece in any den or office. Package also includes a Certificate of Authenticity, Commemorative Publication, and two action photos (Browns & Indians).

PERSONALIZED PLAQUE (#101B) - $89 PLUS TAX/SHIPPING

This 10 by 12 inch plaque can be personalized with the name of your favorite Cleveland fan. The almond colored plaque also includes a 3 by 6 inch section of the "Dawg Pound" scoreboard along with two light bulbs used in the board. Engraved on the plaque is our rendition of Cleveland Stadium. This special memento is designed to be hung on a wall and is a great gift for that long-time Cleveland sports fan. Package also includes a Certificate of Authenticity, Commemorative Publication, and two action photos (Browns & Indians).

LIGHTED SCOREBOARD CABINET (#102B) - $595 PLUS TAX/SHIPPING

Now, for the serious collector, own a piece of the "Dawg Pound" scoreboard that actually lights! We have mounted a 1 by 2 foot section in a custom crafted wood laminated cabinet. The cabinet has a height of 30 inches, width of 22 inches, and a depth of 13 inches. The 32 light section of the scoreboard is attached to a 10 foot power cord which can plug into any household socket. We have also installed a dimmer device to control the brightness of the lights. Only 500 units are being produced and each unit will include its own unique lot number. This limited edition item is designed to be placed on a table top or sturdy shelf. Package includes a Certificate of Authenticity and a 136 page publication about the history of Cleveland Stadium.

HOW TO ORDER
> By Phone
>> Call 1-800-917-DAWG
>> 24 hours a day - 7 days a week
> By Internet
>> Visit our site at wwwdawgone.com and place your order via the World Wide Web.

SHIPPING
> All plaque orders are shipped via US Postal Service Priority Mail, please allow 10-14 days for delivery. The lighted cabinets are produced upon receipt of order, please allow 4 to 6 weeks for delivery.

QUESTIONS/ORDERING INFORMATION
> If you have any other questions, feel free to call us at 1-216-943-0243
> or write us at Stadium Memories, PO Box 595, Willoughby, OH 44096.

STADIUM
MEMORIES

Baseball.
Rock 'n Roll.

Everywhere you

look Cleveland is

consolidating the

old and the new.

The traditional

and the forward

thinking. We share

that philosophy.

Pre-press.
Printing
Fulfillment.
Mailing.

CONSOLIDATED GRAPHICS GROUP, INC.
ROBERT SILVERMAN DIRECT MARKETING DIVISION

"You'll see the difference"